The Career Change Guide

About the author

Rachel Schofield is a qualified personal development and career coach and a former journalist. She worked for the BBC for over twenty years, including reporting for Radio 4's *Woman's Hour* and presenting on the BBC News channel before making her own career pivot into coaching.

Connecting her journalism and her coaching is a deep curiosity for people and their stories and a desire to effect change. She supports clients from senior leaders to women returners to get unstuck, take action and reshape their working lives.

She lives in London with her husband and two teenage daughters. *The Career Change Guide* is her first book.

The Career Change Guide

Five Steps to Finding
Your Dream Job

Rachel Schofield

MICHAEL JOSEPH

PENGUIN MICHAEL JOSEPH

UK | USA | Canada | Ireland | Australia
India | New Zealand | South Africa

Penguin Michael Joseph is part of the Penguin Random House group of companies
whose addresses can be found at global.penguinrandomhouse.com

Penguin
Random House
UK

First published 2023

002

Set in Dante MT Pro, 12.25/16 pt
Printed and bound in Great Britain by Clays Ltd, Elcograf S.p.A.

The authorized representative in the EEA is Penguin Random House Ireland,
Morrison Chambers, 32 Nassau Street, Dublin D02 YH68

A CIP catalogue record for this book is available from the British Library

ISBN: 978–0–241–57636–6

www.greenpenguin.co.uk

For my own band of career change cheerleaders, Jeremy, Martha and Anna, who believed in me when my courage wobbled.

And for any other mums who sometimes need reminding who they really are and what they are capable of.

Contents

Introduction

So tell me, just how long have you been thinking about a career redesign?

A few months? A couple of years? A decade?!

Does it sneak up on you on holiday when your mind finally has time to wander? After a crappy day in the office when you've sold more pointless widgets and your ideas have gone unnoticed? When your surly teen rolls their eyes at yet another meal you've slaved over and you wonder if it's time you went back to work? As you hit 'Like' on a friend's LinkedIn post and notice an uncomfortable twinge of jealousy?

Of course, we all have days when we idly dream of a new life. But this is different.

The career thoughts and ideas that regularly rattle around your brain inspire, terrify and muddle you all at the same time.

You've probably tried the patience of your partner and friends with your constant talk of change and your utter inability to take action.

You've made a few half-hearted attempts to get started but soon backed off, full of more doubt and questions than excitement and motivation.

You've become a serial googler of training courses, solo-preneurs or career pivots.

Sound familiar?

If you're wondering how the A-level choices you made ten years ago have led you down a career path you feel you never really chose . . . if you're reassessing your future now you're a parent with new priorities and different ambitions . . . if you're sensing an opportunity to reinvent yourself as your kids are growing up and it's finally 'you' time . . . if the global pandemic has shaken your world and is pushing you towards change . . . this book is for you.

The wonderful people I coach all have their own individual career stories, but it's fair to say they have three things in common:

- They feel they've somehow lost sight of who they really are.
- They want to create a working life that feels meaningful and fulfilling, but they're unsure what that looks like or how to get there.
- They're excited and motivated some days, and hit by rocky confidence and self-doubt the next.

Sound like you? Thought so.

Because my knowledge of what goes on in the heads of career changers doesn't just come from working with my clients. It comes from my own personal experience of the strange roller-coaster ride that is a career change.

Let me briefly share my story with you.

Before making my very own career pivot, I reported and presented for the BBC for over twenty years. Starting out as a keen young reporter for local TV and radio, I moved to Radio 4's *You and Yours* and *Woman's Hour* and then spent more than a decade presenting for the organization's flagship 24-hour news channel.

I was full-time, part-time and freelance, changing my work to fit around our family and reassessing what worked (and what didn't!) after both of my year-long maternity leaves. I'm married and our two daughters are now teenagers.

When it felt like there was too much that wasn't working – practically and in terms of my own job fulfilment – I did what you're doing. I started investigating. I knew I wasn't inspired. I was fed up with antisocial shifts and felt a little bit unseen as a small freelancer in a huge machine. I knew I still enjoyed asking questions, analysing responses and digging for truth, but I was tired of asking questions people tried to avoid answering and was looking for something more collaborative to replace the combative nature of political debate. I knew I wanted a change – and it needed to be bigger than working as a journalist in another guise. But I was also scared of getting it wrong and parting company with an internationally respected organization which I'd been proud to call home since I was 21.

What else *could* I do with the skills I had? What *should* I do? What did I *want* to do? How would I make it happen? And – horror of horrors – *how would I explain it* in a way that was credible to other people?

Working that out took time, energy and honesty. It led me to where I am now – a fully qualified personal development and career coach, using the techniques and framework I was trained in and my own journey to support others.

But first, I had to do exactly what I'm about to help you to do. Deal with all the negative voices in my own head. Figure out who I really was – in my case after two children and two decades in one industry. Get clear on my purpose. Work out which of my ideas made most sense and felt most promising. Transition from one role to another.

For me, that meant embarking on some formal retraining,

rebranding myself and establishing and growing my own coaching business.

I'm delighted to accompany you on this journey and find out what it means for you.

This book is designed to take you from the confusion and indecision that stops you doing anything to a clearer picture of the kind of work and life you actually want, and then to give you a roadmap to make it a reality.

It will take you on a structured five-step career redesign journey: Preparing – Reflecting – Imagining & Designing – Taking Action – Keeping Going.

First, we'll get your fickle brain in gear and equip you to become a committed career redesigner.

Then you'll reflect on your greatest strengths and skills, what lights you up and what motivates you, to get clear on what meaningful and satisfying work is going to look like for you.

Thirdly, you'll generate and prioritize ideas and explore the resulting career options, designing ways to put them to the test.

Next you'll create a proper action plan for whatever future you decide on.

And you'll finish by supercharging your mindset to ensure you see it through, with insights and advice from people who have already made their own career changes, great or small.

Each step is packed with thought-provoking exercises to increase your self-awareness, clarity and confidence, along with practical insights on how to tackle the day-to-day challenges of a career redesign.

OK, enough procrastination . . . are you ready to discover your dream job?

Step One
Preparing

Before we start, there are a few things we need to tackle head-on.

Because I suspect you've made a few attempts to start this journey before. And you've become stuck. You've felt demoralized. You've run out of steam. So let's make sure that, this time, you pack the right kit for what can at times feel like a bumpy journey. It's tempting to skip this bit. 'Let's just get stuck in!' I hear you thinking. But that's where you've gone wrong before. So trust me, and stick with it.

Chapter 1
Time to Get Off Your But

If there's one massive obstacle in your way, it's you.

Or more specifically, your own brain. It's like you're in a tug of war with yourself. On one side is your ambitious, creative, adventurous self, pulling hard towards change and nurturing thoughts of a more fulfilling work life. Yanking back is your risk-averse, status-quo-loving alter ego, fearful of the unknown and desperate to keep you safe and comfortable.

For every idea you tug at, your brain pulls back control with a big list of why it JUST. WON'T. WORK. The result of this epic tug of war? Your dreams lose. You're forever falling on your but:

'I'd love to return to the arts, but . . .'

'I sometimes wonder if I could start my own business, but . . .'

'I dream of becoming an accountant, but . . .' (OK, so no one has ever said that to me . . . yet)

So what's going on?

Predominantly, our own biology. Neuroscientists will tell you that we're hardwired to resist uncertainty – so much so that our brain prefers a predictable, negative outcome over an uncertain one. Our natural default is to stay put – where our brain is confident it knows what's coming and how to handle it.

No wonder you have a tendency to conclude a career move would be a disaster and jog on, rather than wrestle with the unknown.

Change is certainly challenging. It can seem scary and risky. A career change or redesign doubly so, tied up as it is with our identity and our status, our finances, our family life and our friendships.

'Nope!' says your brain. 'Let's just not go there . . .'

Bored and unchallenged you may be. But at least you're *safe*. Because safety is one of your brain's main priorities. However, in the relative comfort of the twenty-first century, your well-meaning mind has a habit of miscalibrating danger.

'Negativity bias' is a stubborn psychological tendency which served humans well when we were threatened by huge hairy predators with large tusks or sharp teeth. Put simply, you were more likely to survive if your brain was quick to highlight and react to danger and risk. But whilst sabre-toothed tigers no longer routinely jump out at us from behind trees, our brains have been slow to evolve. Have you ever noticed how the one bad experience from your day weighs heavily on your mind as you lie in bed, despite the many positive ones? How one piece of negative feedback knocks the good ones out of the picture? Not all emotions are created equal.

Understanding that your own brain might not be your most reliable companion on this career journey is a powerful realization and one you'll need to return to time and time again. Ready to address the imbalance?

Let's start with that voice inside your head.

Whether you call it your inner critic, your self-saboteur, your sh*tty committee or your confidence gremlin, you'll know what I mean. Even titans like Michelle Obama and Tom Hanks have talked about the experience of self-doubt, so you're in good company. It's natural.

So how do you push back against the brain chatter that's

getting in the way of your career move? We need to get you off your but.

Among the people I work with, I see some really big ones. See if you recognize any of these:

Common Career Change Buts

I've left it too late	It might not suit the family	I'm too old to be taken seriously
I don't have the right skills	I lack the experience	It's not the perfect time
I'd have to take a pay cut	Retraining would take years	I'd have to start at the bottom again

How to Get Off Your But

The key to getting off your but is not to try and ignore its hefty size! Pretending those worries aren't there won't make them go away. So let's grab hold of them, bring them out of the shadows and engage in a spot of truth-tussling.

(⊥)   (⊥)

My Biggest Buts
Complete the following sentence to identify
any negative thoughts that are holding you back.
I'd love to redesign my career BUT . . .

_____

_____

_____

_____

_____

_____

Now what? Well, first it's crucial to understand that you have the ability to separate yourself from your own thoughts.

Your brain is not you. It's offering you a series of beliefs about your career move, but how you respond to them remains in your control. I use the word beliefs deliberately because what your brain is presenting are generally exactly that. Beliefs, not facts. And it's no surprise that the beliefs you've written down are routinely referred to as 'limiting beliefs', because by holding on to them as truths, we stop ourselves growing and progressing towards our goals.

Take this example that I often hear, and you may well have chosen too: 'I'm too old.'

Now that is not a fact, though you may have started to accept it as one. When it comes to your age, there's only one fact in play: the date on your birth certificate. But what your brain has done is take a fact and layer on an *assumption*: that your age makes you 'too old'.

The same often goes for 'I don't have the right skills' or 'The family can't manage without me'. A whole bundle of assumptions are colourfully gift-wrapped by your brain as accepted facts.

So first thank your brain for offering you these thoughts to consider. Remember, it's got your best interests at heart – low risk, safety, security.

But now it's time to launch your investigation.

Take each career-related belief you've doggedly held on to and get it under the magnifying glass. Here are some questions for you to consider:

Belief

How long have I held this belief?
Where does it come from?
What real evidence do I have for this belief?
What other evidence is there?
How does it help me to hold this belief?
How would it help me to let go of it?

Digging into where a belief has come from can be intriguing territory.

Some beliefs we adopted years ago. How many of us have been trotting out the line that we're 'not great with figures' just because A-level maths was never on the table? Or 'I can't give presentations' because we had one awkward run-in with PowerPoint as a junior sales assistant fifteen years ago? It's time to reassess.

Janette – a 47-year-old police officer turned furniture creator – is a case in point.

'There is a bit of sadness. What could I have achieved had I done this a lot sooner? I think one of my big passions

is around how your opportunities and experiences at
school really form what you go on to do in later life. I still
remember my art teacher laughing at me, telling me I wasn't
very creative. And actually, since then, I had never done
anything and it was only really in lockdown that I picked
up a paintbrush. I mean, I'd done DIY, but now I'm kicking
myself because I just wish I could have tuned into my creativity more as a child and I might have done something totally
different.'

More recent beliefs can be equally telling. If you're hampered
by concerns about poor confidence or questionable competence,
you may find that's directly related to how long you've been
toiling in a job that doesn't stimulate or suit you, or perhaps
how long you've been out of the workplace on a career break.
So it's not that you aren't a confident person or your skills have
somehow left the building never to return. It's more than likely
that you simply feel undervalued, out of practice or worried
about a move to a less familiar environment. All of which can be
rectified.

Identifying where a belief has come from can be powerful
too. Sometimes that can be a parent or a teacher. Maybe an
uneasy relationship with a previous boss? Are you really ready to
let them have the last say on your future?

The evidence we have for many of our beliefs is anecdotal
at best. Perhaps it was a conversation we overheard about
the challenges of getting into PR, one article we read about
retraining as a teacher or a quick Google search about the average
age of hairdressers. Hardly concrete data on which to base an
opinion. And yet we do.

And, of course, our negativity bias tends to supercharge that
one piece of worrying 'evidence' over other experiences that

might redress the balance. So remind yourself of times in your life that tell a different story about you, look out for wider success stories and examples of people who have done what you want to do.

It's vital to understand how holding these beliefs is impacting on you. Weirdly, there's normally a pay-off to holding some of these ideas. They help you off the hook and keep you far away from the perceived risk of judgement and humiliation. Of course you can't be expected to make progress in your career when you're 'too old'! How can it be worth trying if 'no one will take me seriously'? These beliefs help you avoid getting uncomfortable.

But the overwhelming impact of these beliefs is to dash your self-belief and stop you before you've really started. How different would your life be if you could let them go? What would change for the better? How would you feel about yourself?

So how firm is your 'but' looking now you've taken a good look? I hope it's all kinds of wobbly.

The next step is to put something more positive and punchy in its place. So that when your fickle brain returns to the 'but', you'll be ready.

'Reframing' negative beliefs is a great habit to develop. Even a simple change of vocabulary can help for starters. If I bring you a 'problem', that's pretty demoralizing, right? If I offer you a 'challenge' or a 'puzzle' not so much, even though it might still prove hard.

So how else could you look at that belief when it shows up? What alternative perspectives could you adopt? And what could be the result of you shifting your thinking?

Here are a couple of examples:

Managing Your Mindset
REFRAMING

Current Belief	Other Perspectives	Result
I can't do this without letting other people in the family down.	*It's OK to ask the family to make some changes and for everyone to play their part.*	*Move away from feelings of guilt. Take action to share household chores more fairly.*
It's too late to make a career change.	*I have years of experience to offer and another 25 years of work still to shape!*	*Greater motivation and self-belief. An end to continual procrastination.*

Try it for yourself.

Managing Your Mindset
REFRAMING

Current Belief	Other Perspectives	Result

Rest assured, this is not some trite exercise in sugar-coating. When you've taken a good look, you may come to the conclusion that some beliefs you hold, some of the buts holding you back, are indeed closer to facts. It may be the case that you don't have a particular qualification. That the local nursery will be expensive to send your kids to if you change your hours. That you are slightly lousy at interviews. It may be fair to say that you are short on relevant experience. That a pay cut would be challenging.

In which case, dare I point out that sitting on that but still won't help you! The question becomes not one of reframing but: What you are going to *do* about it? Some career buts are a total deal-breaker. If you want to join the police force and you're 58, chances are that's a waste of time, as you'll have to retire at 60. If you want to be a doctor but aren't up for six years plus of study, it's game over. But there are very few scenarios like that in reality.

If this exercise has thrown up practical barriers you're still worried may get in your way, make a note of them. Checking the truth of them will form part of your investigations in Chapter 9. Because chances are, they can be worked on, particularly if you're prepared to think laterally. Relevant experience can be built up, poor interview skills can be improved, qualifications can be fine-tuned or sometimes circumvented, alternative childcare arrangements can be found.

I hope you're seeing how crucial your mindset is going to be to this process. But let me stress at this point, that this is not a case of one 10-minute exercise and you've got it nailed.

You may well be pushing back against default patterns of thinking about your work life that have been established for many years. These beliefs have become well-worn neural pathways in your brain, forming foundations for habits in the way you think and feel and, consequently, behave. Put simply, the flattened grass and deep indentations make it very easy for your brain to keep walking you down these routes. And every time you walk down them, you embed the habit even more. The path less trodden – perhaps that you have great abilities or are a serious candidate or feel strong and confident – is harder for your brain to spot.

The good news is that your brain can develop new pathways.

Neuroplasticity is the ability of the brain to adapt and change in response to new information, experiences or environments. On this career redesign journey, it's your job to feed your brain those new stimuli! You have in your kit one hell of a powerful tool. Make it your daily habit to challenge your old thinking and be open to the new.

Key Takeaways

Your brain is hardwired to dislike change and uncertainty and is not always a reliable indicator of how possible a career change can be.

Negativity bias supercharges our observations of what seems risky, dangerous or troubling.

Many of our thoughts are beliefs not facts. Examining where they come from and how true they are is vital.

It's possible for your brain to develop new ways of thinking, known as neural pathways, if you work at it.

Action Checklist

☐ I have identified my biggest mindset barriers and reframed the negative thoughts my brain is offering me about my career change

☐ I have made a note of any practical challenges I genuinely believe may impact my ability to change career

Chapter 2
The Three Cs

So you've owned up to the size of your but and decided to finally give it a good kicking. You've accepted your brain may need some ongoing encouragement on this journey if it's not going to derail you. But – I'm sorry to tell you – there are other potential pitfalls heading your way.

Don't worry, I'm very big on encouragement as well, but I like to tell it how it is. Because have you noticed how the world of fridge magnets and car stickers is trying to trick you into thinking a career redesign will be a breeze?

'If you can dream it, you can do it!'

'Let your dreams be your wings!'

Wow. Just let me sit down with a coffee and imagine my best life and I'm almost there. Who knew?

Ah, if only. By all means, make that cuppa and grab a seat. But we're not dreaming yet. (Though we definitely will, I promise.) First, though, I'm going to talk you through the Three Cs. Without them, you can dream all you like but I suspect it won't happen.

The Three Cs

Commitment   Courage   Curiosity

1. Commitment

A career change is not the work of five minutes and it's not always easy. You've got to be ready to stick with it. Give it proper time, focus and energy. This could take many months; it could take a year. Maybe more if you are aiming for something excitingly radical. Are you ready for that?

If you've been procrastinating over this for quite a while, occasionally going at it in a slightly half-arsed manner, you should be getting a hot wave of recognition right now.

What was it Thomas Edison said? 'Opportunity is missed by most people because it is dressed in overalls and looks like work.'

In fact, I'd encourage you to think of it exactly like that. Reshaping your career is best approached as a mini job in itself. Which might sound like a bit of a bummer, because in this case no one will be paying you, the office doesn't have aircon and there's no fancy coffee machine. But you do get to choose your own holidays and you can have as many Dress-Down Fridays and Doughnut Days as you want.

Consider yourself in charge of a creative work project. The plan is for it to be fun, but yes, it's going to take proper Commitment.

So just like a job, you'll need to put some structure in place. Create some effective routines, prioritize your tasks and have the right team around you to ensure you can do your best work and achieve your goals.

Create an Effective Routine

There will be days when you're raring to go on Project New You and days when you're just not feeling it. What you are aiming for here is consistency. Flurries of activity followed by weeks of inaction is a deeply ineffective way to make progress and a sure-fire way to lose momentum.

This book is packed with exercises and challenges to get you started and set you on your way. Get into good habits with scheduling these and you will lay some great foundations for keeping going and finally bringing about the change you so desperately want.

So, let's nail down the practicalities that will be best for you. As with everything I'm going to ask you to do, there is no right answer. This journey is yours and it's vital you take ownership of it. So – depending on your current situation – you may have five hours a week to give to this process, you may have two hours a fortnight. The important thing is you decide what feels manageable and stick to it.

How much time do I want to dedicate to my career change each week?

When and where do I work best?

How will I make and keep my notes?

TIP: What feels manageable but also motivating? Are you a little-and-often person (30 minutes a day) or someone who focuses better with a big chunk of time (every Monday evening)?

TIP: Play to your strengths: what time of the day do you do your best thinking? What kind of environment suits you – do you have a favourite spot in the house or is it better to escape to a coffee shop or the local library where there's less distraction?

TIP: Don't end up with a muddle of scrappy notes you can't later decipher! Do you like to work digitally or by hand? Will a fresh new notebook inspire you or are you an Excel spreadsheet geek?

Once you've decided on the time commitment you want to make, grab your diary and ring-fence those time slots as fixed appointments with yourself. Call it 'Project Me' or 'Job Power Hour' or whatever feels motivating and real. I'm serious. Do it.

If you don't protect this process, other things will creep in and it will be the first thing that falls off your agenda. Which leads me to your need to . . .

Prioritize

I suspect your own future plans come pretty low down the pecking order, particularly if you currently have caring responsibilities.

We can feel like we have endless demands on our time. As colleagues, partners, parents, children, siblings or friends, we have hefty to-do lists whether inside or outside work. Caring responsibilities can fall particularly heavily on women. Whether your work is paid, voluntary or household, you may feel you are carrying a huge mental load. If I were to take a screen grab of your brain right now, would I find a crazed jumble of dentist appointments, unanswered emails, in-laws' birthdays, school reply slips, gym guilt, car MOTs and passport renewals *on top* of any other work you have do?

Consider this career project a chance to step back and reflect on your life and commitments more widely. In order to give this adventure the time it deserves, indeed, the time *you* deserve, there are things that might need to change. And not just in the short term while you work your way through this book.

This is a great opportunity to do a quick audit of your time and your commitments. Whether you are already working in a formal capacity or a member of the small army of people holding up their families and communities (or both), I'll bet you have 101 extra demands cropping up.

I'm not saying you need to ditch these commitments, but some will feel like important, conscious choices you've made and others will be habits, activities or roles you've fallen into and might need to reconsider. Remember, this process is the start of a bigger change, and reclaiming control of your own time will build you some strong foundations for the future you.

Take a look at your average week and how you're spending your time. Use the following questions to help you assess whether your own career redesign is going to survive an encounter with your current reality:

- List the people or activities that currently make calls on your time. What might you need to say No to if you are going to say Yes to this new chapter of your life?

- List all the things that are likely to stop you sticking to your career appointments, such as last-minute work demands, invitations to see an old friend, the needs of your mum-in-law or children's sports fixtures. How will you handle these?

- Think of your home and family. How would you assess the current balance of responsibilities? What conversations need to happen to bring about any change you feel is needed? What would you like your partner and children to do that they aren't currently doing?

- What additional resources or help could you call on to give you more time and headspace? Think about arranging some reciprocal playdates for your kids with a friend, asking your teenager to walk the dog, using an afterschool club or switching to an online shop and batch cooking for the freezer.

Build Your Team

Career redesign can feel like a lonely journey at times so having some walking companions will serve you well. But beware – other people can be both a blessing and a curse. Some people are going to inspire and encourage you. Others, often with kind intent, will walk up to your dreams with a big bucket of cold water and dump it all over them. The key is the ability to spot the difference. So let's choose your supporters wisely.

Oddly, some well-meaning family and friends may be your worst allies. They can be desperate to help 'fix' you, throwing constant advice at you without really listening to what you want and getting frustrated when you don't act on it. Which simply adds to your muddle and overwhelm. Or perhaps they attempt to solve your dilemma with one assured opinion on what you *obviously* need to do, failing to acknowledge the range of other things you're contemplating. Or they lovingly bash you over the head with a helpful dose of 'realism' about how difficult it will be.

Take Dave, who at 35 wanted to leave his career in the travel industry and make a move into software programming.

'I remember my old boss, who's actually a really good friend of mine, took me out for lunch on my last day. And she pretty much said, "Well, I'll see you in a year, the door's always open. I don't mean this in a bad way, but I don't think this is the right move for you and I suspect you'll be back. But good on you for giving it a go." And I think that actually drove me even more, I was so determined to prove them wrong. There was no way I was ever going back to travel and I would never crawl back through the door and say, "Can I have my job back?"'

It was Dave's wife who became his best career change companion, as you'll see if you read his whole story in Chapter 12: Reflections from Career Changers.

Sam, who became a charity worker after leaving a 20-year teaching career, also had to wrestle with the weight of well-intentioned but difficult opinions.

'I'd worked in my local area for a very long time. So I know a lot of people and when they all found out I was leaving, they were shocked, and I felt as if I was letting them down, disappointing them. They'd say, "But why are you leaving teaching? You're a brilliant teacher!" I know that if my parents were alive they would have been really disappointed because they were so, so proud of their daughter going to university and being a teacher, that was a huge thing. I've got to be honest, I struggled with that, even though I knew I didn't want to be teaching.'

Why does this happen? Well, consider this . . . your family and friends, rather like your brain, want to keep you safe. After all, they love you. And they can be particularly risk-averse on your behalf when it comes to change. And – dare we say it – possibly on their own behalf too. After all, you may be the lynchpin of the family and if you shake things up, it's likely to have an impact on them too. They have skin in the game and that can complicate their approach, even if only subconsciously.

Remember, your family and friends have known you for a very long time. Long ago, they neatly processed, boxed and labelled you. To them, personally, you are 'always-available mum', 'fun partner', 'bossy big brother', 'wild party-giver'. Professionally, they have you nailed too – teacher, account manager, PA, lawyer . . . So when you decide it's time to rewrite those labels, is it any surprise their mental computer sometimes says no? They may find it hard to envisage you in a different role, and unintentionally they hold you back with their brain's lack of imagination.

Freddie, who changed from acting to nursing, urges caution in the early stages of a career shift.

'Your story is yours to tell and only tell as much of it as you want to. And if you're not ready to tell it, don't tell it. You can say, "Well, actually, I'm looking at new options now. And I'm in the middle of having a rethink," and I think maybe that kind of language is easier for people to understand.'

You're not obliged to offer a running commentary on your career redesign to all and sundry. Follow your instinct. Who will help and who might hinder?

Here are some pointers:

Seek Encouragers

- Who are the people that buoy you up and motivate you?
- Who are the glass-half-fullers in your life?
- Who tends to see adventure before risk?

Seek Questioners

- Who are the people who listen more than talk?
- Who is more likely to ask interesting questions than offer advice or opinions?
- Who in your life tends to use phrases like 'If I were you . . .', 'The way I see it is . . .', 'What you want to do is . . .'? Avoid where possible!

Seek Accountability Partners

- Who could help ensure you stay committed to investigating a new career? Who could you see regularly as a way of keeping on track?
- How could you build in some accountability, such as sending them a weekly WhatsApp message to tell them what you've done and what progress you've made?
- Is there a career-redesigning friend you could buddy up with to work through the exercises in this book and undertake this journey together? Sometimes all you need is an accountability partner to make sure you stick with it!

So now you've established some ways to power up your Commitment to your career redesign. What else will you need?

2. Courage

Let me put this out here right now. Over the course of this journey, your confidence is going to wobble. Your inner critic is going to go to town. You're going to encounter setbacks and feel demoralized and frustrated. Rest assured, that is *totally normal*.

Crucially, you'll need to get uncomfortable at times, challenge yourself and take some risks.

When I moved away from journalism and started retraining as a coach, I regularly had moments of thinking it was all too hard and would never work. It was weird and unsettling to be a beginner at something again after so many years of operating in a world that was reassuringly familiar. I was gradually becoming less focused on my BBC work, but I wasn't fully a coach yet. I was stuck in the discomfort of a 'liminal space' and that's where you're heading. In fact, you might already feel you're there.

The word liminal comes from the Latin '*limen*', meaning threshold, a place where you enter or leave, a place of transition. Liminal spaces can be literal, physical places – think airports, train stations, stairwells, hotel lobbies, doctors' waiting rooms.

You know that strange feeling those places evoke of being slightly tense or unsettled? That's the emotional or psychological aspect of liminal spaces and it shows up strongly at times of change or transformation. Life changes like starting university, becoming a parent, divorce, moving house or bereavement. You're on the verge of something new but not yet there. Waiting for news or at the start of a new chapter but uncertain quite what it will bring.

Psychologically, a career redesign is a corker of a liminal space. You are leaving the old but not yet clear on the new. You are in-between, and it can play havoc with your sense of identity.

When Freddie decided to leave acting in his early thirties, he initially struggled with the change.

'We do live in a world where a great deal of our validation and self-worth comes from the work that we do and that's because we spend a lot of time doing it. If you can't give a name to what you want to do, you are immediately a slightly alien presence in a room, when most other people can, and that's a difficult space to occupy when you're changing careers. Because, of course, often there's no short answer, and people really are sort of asking for the short answer.'

You can hear more from Freddie on page 300.
If that makes you fearful or unsettled, here are some things to

consider, because liminal spaces should feel powerful and exciting as well as occasionally perilous!

- Liminal spaces are as much about looking forwards as looking backwards. Rather than worry about what you may be letting go of, keep reminding yourself of the possibility and opportunity on the other side. This can help fight your natural urge to step backwards towards the familiar.
- Be accepting of the tension or discomfort. This is a process of transformation, after all. And without getting too clichéd with talk of snakes shedding their skin or caterpillars transforming into butterflies, the mess is where the magic happens. Seriously. I will tell you more than once in this book that it's getting stuck into that 'muddle in the middle' that will be fundamental to your success.

But how to do that?

Tap into the Power of Your Why

There will be moments when you wonder why you're bothering with this at all, and your courage and energy start to falter. In order to keep going, it's vital to have a powerful Why – a compelling, exciting and motivating reason for making your shift.

Here's Kerys, a journalist who became a teacher:

'I really valued, and really wanted to be an equal contributor to, the family – that was a real driving force for me. I also wanted to have something for me. I think I want to be good at something. I want to have my own identity.'

Stuart, who made a shift out of media law, puts it this way:

'I wanted a career that I found more fulfilling, that I could get passionate about, that I could feel was worthwhile and meaningful. It felt important to me to do something that helps people and is useful to society. I'm willing to work hard, but I need to care about what I'm doing. I much prefer the idea of a vocation to a job.'

Joanne, a cleaner who went on to qualify as a children's nurse in her forties, could trace her Why to her own experience growing up.

'I was bored cleaning and I thought I could do more. I lost my mum, she died when I was 21. So that maybe had an influence. She'd been a stay-at-home mum. And she'd had a couple of tries at going out to work. She was originally a hairdresser, and then she'd got a job in Marks and Spencer but she only lasted a day, she couldn't do it. I think she felt a bit worthless and I didn't want to be like Mum, waiting for my husband to come home from work every day. To put his tea on the table. My mum did that and I didn't want that. I think that's probably my motivation.'

Before you start down this road for yourself, let's take a moment to get really clear on what this journey is all about for you. We're aiming to create a one-paragraph vision you can draw on in your wobbly moments. I urge you to write down your answers to each question overleaf before finalizing your paragraph, rather than attempting to answer the questions in your head. Research shows that the process of writing things down, particularly by hand, helps your brain process and retain thoughts more fully.

Answer these questions:

- What is really important to you about making a change to your work life?
- What difference will a career redesign make to your life as a whole?
- What will it give you that you don't have now?

Now take yourself into a future where you have achieved the career shift you want. Really imagine yourself there.

- How will you be feeling? What will you be saying to yourself? What will other people be saying to you? How will things be different?
- And, crucially, how will you be feeling a year from now, if you don't give it your full commitment?

Write out your Why and stick it in the front of your notebook, on a Post-it note on the fridge or tuck it into your wallet or purse. Revisit it regularly to help keep you on track.

Cultivate Your Growth Mindset

I'm guessing if you've had a child at school over the last ten years, you'll have heard teachers talk about helping them develop a 'growth' rather than a 'fixed' mindset. Stanford University psychologist Carol Dweck contends that our own attitude to our ability is crucial for us to make real progress, and I'd suggest that the same is true for your career redesign.

Put simply, with a fixed mindset, people believe that their talent and abilities are innate gifts and tend to overlook the impact of effort and learning on their success. They believe their 'natural' skills are set, meaning they rarely stray into difficult or unfamiliar territory where they might fail. Whereas with a growth mindset, your brains and talent are merely the starting point. You believe that you can develop through hard work, good strategies and input from others, and consequently – asserts Dweck – you can achieve far more.

What I love about this – and I'd encourage you to embrace it too – is Dweck's resulting call for us to set out expecting to make mistakes, to step into scenarios that stretch us and to be OK about not being able to do something 'yet'. Cultivating your growth mindset means realizing that you are learning even when things don't turn out how you imagined or the first outcome is not a triumph.

It's a brilliant approach to this journey, where there may be some quirky detours, unforeseen barriers or occasional dead-ends.

Everything you try has something valuable to teach you, even if you might feel like an idiot at times. Which leads me to . . .

3. Curiosity

To get the most from the exercises and theories in this book, you need to make Curiosity your best friend.

I'll be getting you to *answer* a lot of questions I've devised, but what I really want is for you to become brilliant at *asking* your own questions too – of yourself and, later, of other people (yep, I'm afraid you heard that right).

It may feel counter-intuitive, but a career change is initially far less about the end destination and much more about the journey.

The biggest revelations will appear along the way. So dial down the pressure. Quit obsessing about exactly where you're heading and get curious about what you're encountering on the way.

Here are eight approaches to cultivate Curiosity. You'll see many of these crop up in specific exercises throughout the book, but if you start embedding them now, you will be building your very own coaching toolkit. Dip back into this section regularly as you undertake the work, when you need inspiration or some help deciphering what's going on for you.

1. Go Below

The key to getting maximum insight from your answers is to try to go a little deeper. Your first thoughts may feel like a big bowl of cake mixture, all messy egg yolks, dusty flour and gloopy butter. What you need to develop is the ability to visualize the tasty sponge cake that could emerge.

Here are some simple additional questions that can be powerful at unearthing useful insights about yourself after any exercise. When you're reflecting on what you've written, try asking yourself:

- What might that be telling me?
- How significant does that feel? Or not?
- What has surprised me about that?
- What difference does this make?

2. What's in a Word?

As a coach, I'm trained to listen very carefully to a client's choice of words. And to be curious about what different words mean to different people. What I mean by 'interesting' or 'dull' or 'fulfilling' may be quite unlike what you mean.

So get specific about what you mean, push yourself to define important words more clearly and look out for words that seem especially powerful for you or keep cropping up.

Pay particular notice when you find yourself thinking or saying 'I should' or 'I ought to'. They can often indicate that you are operating from a place of doubt, guilt, pressure or other people's expectations rather than what you really want to do. Definitely a mini alarm bell for you to listen out for.

3. Pattern Spotting

On which note, an idea, word or attribute that comes up once may not be hugely significant. What you want to get curious about are the patterns and themes that start emerging. Where are the important common threads appearing in your past, present and future? Having a couple of highlighters to hand during exercises is a great way to start capturing important recurring ideas or concepts. It's helpful to look back over what you write with eagle eyes and highlight any words that you tend to repeat.

4. Bring All Your Brains

Scientists tell us that we actually have *three* brains – head, heart and gut – each with their own neurons and neurotransmitters, and the ability to take in, process and store information.

Your head is your rational brain, searching out and organizing facts, measuring risks, assessing pros and cons. This brain deals in what logic says you ought to do.

Your heart is your emotional brain, interpreting the world through passion and feelings. Thinking with this brain is about what you want or don't want to do. It helps you process whether you feel hot or cold about an idea, excited or flat.

Your gut is your intuitive brain. Its messages aren't always crystal clear, but they give us a sense if something feels right or feels off. This brain deals with instincts.

Since the time of the Ancient Greeks, Western philosophy has historically prized rational thought – thinking with our heads and basing our conclusions on reason rather than emotion. Consequently, some of us feel we should try to take emotion and instinct out of our decision-making processes.

But to stay curious, why not play around with all three of your brains? If you know you tend to make decisions based on one particular brain, don't forget to invite the others along to get their perspective.

5. Follow the Energy

Building on that idea of tapping into your own different responses, it's important to really notice when you meet resistance or enthusiasm. Be on the lookout for things that evoke *interesting* responses in you – things that inspire, challenge, excite or even worry you!

If you meet resistance, ask yourself where that's coming from. Get curious about what's in play: is it fear of failure? Doubt about your ability? Those limiting beliefs we talked about? In which case, it's time for a little pushback. On the other hand, the resistance may simply indicate a basic lack of excitement for a particular idea, a realization that this isn't something you really want to pursue now you've got it under the microscope. Pay attention. That's valuable information.

If you meet enthusiasm, be receptive to those little sparks of energy and those flashes of potential. What are they telling you? I'm not necessarily talking about intense passion here. (Later we'll discuss whether searching for that is even a helpful concept.) I'm talking the tiny tingles that tell you something's landed.

6. Time Travel

Chances are you're feeling pretty bogged down in your current life and its limitations. So if you see this process purely through the filter of your rather jaded present self, you'll be missing the wisdom of your past and future selves. When you're considering a career idea, and you hit a potential challenge or you're searching for a different strategy, indulge in a spot of time travel with questions like these:

Ask Yourself

- How would I have approached this twenty years ago?
- What will I feel about this in two weeks? Six months? Five years?
- What would my 75-year-old self say to me about this?
- What does my 21-year-old self have to teach me?
- When have I experienced something like this before?
- Have I always felt like this? What's different now?

7. Play with Perspectives

While you're barrelling through time in your mental Tardis, why not try stepping out of your own body occasionally too and mixing up your viewpoint?

Consider

- How else could I look at that?
- What if I told myself the opposite?

- What would I tell my best friend if she asked my opinion on this?
- How would Sheryl Sandberg/Alan Sugar/the Dalai Lama/the Prime Minister/my granny approach this?

You don't have to choose people you love or admire, just people who might bring a different view to you, often without all the negativity you're carrying! What you're doing with your perspective-shifting is training your brain to think creatively and reject its default settings, which generally come with a big side helping of self-judgement.

8. Think Whole Life

Whilst we're predominantly focused on your work, it's highly likely insights will come up that are valuable to your life as a whole.

You'll be asked to consider what's important to you, what you enjoy, how you want to spend your days and how you define success and fulfilment. These things don't solely belong in your professional world. And expecting to create a career that is the answer to all your needs overlooks the power you have to shape other parts of your life as well – your role in your family, your leisure time, how you think about yourself, how you communicate your needs, where you invest your energy.

As you discover more about yourself, keep checking in with yourself to assess how what you're learning resonates with the rest of your life.

Key Takeaways

A career change takes time and effort.

The best things you can bring to this process are Commitment, Courage and Curiosity.

Being in-between different careers is a kind of liminal space – it's uncomfortable because you are on a threshold between leaving one thing and starting another.

Knowing what is truly important to you about making a career change will be a great source of motivation.

Embracing a growth mindset, where you are prepared to learn, fail and get things wrong, is a massive asset.

Action Checklist

☐ I have ringfenced regular time to work through the steps in this book and identify any potential stumbling blocks to my ability to commit to this exciting journey

☐ I am going to keep clear notes

☐ I have chosen the right team of people to share this journey with

☐ I have written a powerful WHY

☐ I am trying eight new approaches to cultivate curiosity about myself and my career journey

Step Two
Reflecting

Now you've started to tackle your mindset and you've ramped up your Commitment, Courage and Curiosity. Your kitbag is packed. So where should you be heading first?

One of the biggest mistakes I see often is people jump into action too quickly. You're so unhappy in your current work or so keen to regain your working identity that you leap before you look, rush to update your CV, polish your LinkedIn profile and fire off a flurry of random job applications. Wow, you're motoring! Except quite probably in the wrong direction and giving out the wrong message. Because you're moving *away* from something you don't like and not *towards* something you actively want. Your push is much stronger than your pull and the information you're working with is woefully incomplete.

You soon get derailed because you're not actually sure if you're applying for things you really want. And that lack of certainty is picked up by the very people you're trying to convince, meaning you're much less likely to be successful. Rejection letters or radio silence follow, further bashing your confidence. If you do land a new role, you're thrown into an enormous quandary about whether you should take it because you have no real idea if it's right for you. Even among your own friends, family or colleagues, you're not confident talking about what's next and how you see your future, because you don't really know. Which means your messaging lacks conviction, you avoid talking about your plans and you're not in the right place to build the connections and initiate the conversations that could supercharge this process.

Now don't misunderstand me. Action is going to be vital. In fact, the second biggest mistake I see is people not taking any action, but we'll come to that later. So what do I mean by advising you not to dive in too quickly?

Think of it like this. Trying to identify your ideal job is a big ask from a blank page.

Because it's more than words on a name badge – it's a role that pulls together four key things.

In Step Two we'll reflect on those fundamentals:

- What You're Good At
- What's Important to You
- What Interests and Excites You
- How You Want to Work

These are the crucial puzzle pieces in building a vibrant picture of what you want your future career to look like.

You'll explore them through a series of thought-provoking exercises.

At the end of Chapters 3 to 6, I'll prompt you to summarize what they've revealed in the Career Profile opposite. If you want more space, create your own version either on paper or digitally. Revisit and update it regularly as you get to know yourself better.

This information-rich, personalized Career Profile will be a valuable reference point against which to measure your ideas. Invest real time in fine-tuning your profile and you will be much more confident about what you are looking for.

My Career Profile

My Strengths and Skills	My Work Values

My Ideal Work Environment	My Interests

My Definition of Success

Say Hello to Yourself

Before we get into the specific details needed to build your Career Profile, let me warm you up with a big-picture exercise. I want to invite you to gently remind yourself who's looking back at you in the mirror and what they really want.

Identity is a massive issue for a lot of career changers, particularly those who have spent time in an unhappy job or focused on family. Sometimes you're so used to just plodding along, holding things together, that you're no longer sure what will bring you the most satisfaction because it's so long since you stopped to consider who you are. If you've taken a career break, you may well think of your professional self rather like a long-lost relative, whose face is vaguely familiar but whose backstory you struggle to recall with any accuracy.

Whether you're a mum, a mid-lifer or a miserable middle manager, it's time to reconnect with yourself.

So we'll start this reintroduction to your full, glorious, complex self with a personality profile. You can find many of these for free online, and they are generally based on the well-known Myers Briggs Type Indicator (MBTI) created by Isabel Myers and Katharine Briggs in the 1960s. This mother-and-daughter team were inspired by the Swiss psychiatrist Dr Carl Jung and wanted to turn his complex theories on psychological types into accessible, useful information for individuals.

Some people love this kind of questionnaire, but if you're rolling your eyes at this point and muttering about teen magazines, all the better. I'm starting by taking some of you out of your comfort zone and asking you to be curious. And to reassure you, I've lost count of the number of people who came back to me after this exercise saying, 'I was pretty sceptical about doing this, but . . .'

Head to https://www.16personalities.com/ and give it a go. You'll find other examples of this kind of profile in the Resources section at the end of the book. I'm not asking you to take your results as gospel or get bogged down in the minutiae of whether you're an INFJ or an ESFP. This is not about putting you in a box; no personality type is 'better' than another or totally black and white.

I'm inviting you to start training your self-reflection muscles. Put simply, notice what you notice. Be alert to elements that really resonate and feel free to interrogate or disregard anything that doesn't really ring true. See what challenges you or makes you uncomfortable. Look out for valuable insights into your natural strengths and weaknesses, the way you like to work, how you interact with other people and the things that drive you or hold you back. If you find yourself looking at other profiles and deciding you prefer elements of those, ask yourself what that means. Are you getting a better sense of your own reflection?

Now you have an overview, let's get more specific. Over the next four chapters, we're going to dig further into these areas.

Here's my advice on how to use the exercises you'll encounter:

- Approach them with an open mind and see where they lead you. Some you might find easy and enjoyable. Some may prove revelatory. Others could prove challenging or frustrating.
- No one exercise is a magic bullet. There are no right answers and everyone's mind works differently. So if you encounter an exercise that feels unhelpful to you, or you'd rather do in a slightly different way, that's fine.
- I'd encourage you to take your time and, if necessary, return to exercises after you've let them brew for a while.
- Have fun!

Chapter 3
What You're Good At

I recently asked a client to undertake the personality profile you've just tried and to email me a note of what felt most like her before our session. When we met, I pointed out to Hannah what she'd done without even realizing:

> 'You've just sent me all the Weaknesses you agreed with! Where are the Strengths that rang true for you?'

Whether it's due to modesty, negativity bias or a tendency to underplay achievements, we're often far greater experts in our own shortcomings than in our abilities. But working out what you're great at, owning your fantastic abilities, and being able to talk about them convincingly, is going to be vital to this process. Mainly because it's massively valuable data to inform your next move. But also because, at some point, you'll need to share them with other people.

So, first let's get clear on the Strengths and Skills you have. Then we'll identify which ones you most enjoy using or want to develop.

TIP: Digging for Gold

Throughout this process, people often make the mistake of thinking the golden nuggets of information they need are hidden in some magical cave they haven't yet found. In reality, you already have a whole mine of valuable information about yourself, if only you'll make time to grab a spade and dig for it. This is not an abstract process. It's about mining your past and your present to better shape your future.

Unearth Your Strengths

1. Make a list of all the jobs you have had to date,

from your teenage paper round to your most recent job. If you enjoy working visually, you might like to draw a timeline of your career and inset the jobs along it. You can use colours or symbols to mark any particular high points, achievements, periods of fulfilment or even discontent.

2. Dig into the details,

for each job, spend some time reminding yourself of any particular projects you worked on, clients, colleagues or bosses of particular significance, areas of responsibility you had or specific roles you took on. This will give you a clearer picture of the day-to-day work you were doing. Strengths are more potent when they are specific and linked to real-life examples.

3. Answer the following questions for each of those periods of your professional life:

– What do you regard as some of your best achievements (big or small) in that role?
– What abilities or strengths do you think contributed to your success?

– What aspects of each job came easily to you?

– Where did you really shine?

– When there were challenges to overcome,
what strengths and skills did you draw on?

– How did you bring particular value?

– What role do you tend to take in any group/team?

– What made you different to other people?

– What impact did you have on the business/project/group?

The Other Yous

It's easy to narrow your focus at this point and concentrate all your thoughts about your talents and abilities into a work context. But your Strengths show up in all areas of your life. And if you've had a career break of any kind, it can be particularly important to remind yourself of that.

So take some time to consider the other versions of you listed below. You might also like to draw on other times in your life too, perhaps as a student or – if relevant – before you had a partner or children.

Family	Community	Hobbies
Think about the many roles you play as part of your immediate and wider family unit, whether as a partner, parent, sibling, etc. Consider your friendships too.	Think about any voluntary or community work you've done. That might be for a charity, your children's school, your place of worship or a campaign group.	Don't overlook the things you do or used to do in your free time. This can be particularly interesting if you've taken part in group activities or team sports.

Run the same questions again, adapting them to think more in terms of your role than your 'job'.

When you're thinking more holistically about your skill set, there are two other cracking questions to try:

*What kind of tasks do you naturally offer
to do even when you're not being paid?*

And

What do people turn to you for help with?

Are you a great listener? A social media or computer guru? Do friends covet your decorating choices? Ask your advice on their finances or holiday plans? Do you write highly persuasive emails? Chair meetings like a pro?

Playing with Perspectives

Sometimes our Strengths come so naturally to us we tend to undervalue them. That's where other people come in!

Pick five significant people – ideally some of whom know you in a work or semi-professional capacity either currently or historically – and ask each of them to email you what they believe are your three biggest Strengths. Be brave!

Don't put them on the spot but ask them to drop you a line when they've had time to reflect. Encourage them to give you examples of what they are saying. This is an exercise that may fill you with horror. Approach people? Ask them what I'm good at? You've got to be kidding!

But you'll be amazed what comes back.

Here's an email I received from Marta after I set her this task:

'I felt really resistant to doing it and threw my toys out of the pram (mentally!) and decided I didn't have enough people I had worked with to call on and ask and that I couldn't do it. Then I decided I was perhaps being a bit overdramatic and negative about it so I actually asked seven people in the end!'

Don't believe her? Here's Jason:

'I put this out to a few work colleagues. After getting over the awkwardness of sending these requests, receiving the feedback really perked up a rainy Tuesday so I decided to canvass the opinion of my family too! Why not?!'

INSIGHT

The Many Strengths Lurking Inside a Single Word

Here is part of an email exchange I had with Helen after she had asked others for their feedback on her strengths. It's a great example of the 'What's in a Word?' approach I encouraged you to adopt in Chapter 2. Pay attention to your reaction to particular words and get curious about the many ways words can be interpreted:

HELEN: What I found interesting from this was that I found it annoying and disappointing when people said I was kind, thoughtful, etc. I thought it was a 'non' strength. Isn't everyone kind? It all felt a bit wishy-washy. But then it's not like I am a high-powered businesswoman, so I guess most of the qualities are more 'mum' qualities rather than 'work' qualities if you know what I mean . . . Anyway, I found it an interesting exercise as afterwards I felt like I wanted to change those words by doing something new!

ME: I totally hear what you are saying and why you might – on the surface – feel that 'kind' is a rather vague quality.

However, everyone is not kind to the extent that it would be an active strength. Yes, kindness is considered a universal human value in the most basic sense, but I can assure you it's not a quality that would be named as a key one when many people are being described by their friends or colleagues. (I know, because I see a lot of these feedback forms!) I'd invite you to see that your kindness manifests itself in a far more active way, which is why it has surfaced.

Kindness is perhaps the easiest word for summarizing your qualities that your friends have reached for – but think about what concrete skills and strengths underlie that: I suspect (judging by your earlier email this week about how helping others had distracted you from your own plans!) that the word kindness points to a huge range of strengths that you have – empathy, excellent listening skills, high emotional intelligence, great verbal communication, calm under pressure, altruistic, interpersonal skills, practical and emotional problem-solving, etc.

On reflection, you might think those qualities go some way to explaining why you were drawn to teaching and now are considering art therapy. Could it be that those career paths match well to this element of your personality and strengths?

So, that's me inviting you to look a little deeper. Words are interesting and often deserve a bit more unpicking!

But I also hear that you were prickled into wanting to change those words. A great question for you is, what words would you like to come up instead?

Do They See What You See?

How did other people's assessments of your
strengths match your own?

What surprised you? What pleased you?

What have you been failing to see?
Or taking for granted?

What do you notice about how different
groups of people see you?

What words keep recurring? What do you
feel about them?

Did you like the way people see you? What are people
missing? What else do you want them to see? What
would you need to do to change that?

Strengths are traits that feel like part of your character, things
you are naturally good at and probably always have been. Let's
face it, your leadership, resilience or creativity was no doubt
showing up in the playground long before you set foot in an
office! Your Strengths are the deep foundation layer on to which
you have built a skill set, which you have the potential to use,
expand and adapt in any number of ways. As I encouraged Helen
to see, her natural kindness could be broken down into numerous
concrete skills such as listening and problem-solving.

So we should get specific about the kinds of tasks where your
Strengths can really show up and shine. If communication is a
natural strength for you, this could manifest itself in many ways
– strong public speaking, broadcasting or interviewing skills

come to mind. Or you might feel you are more gifted as a written communicator, excelling in report writing, sales pitches or even poetry!

Starring Roles

Below you'll find a set of roles people routinely play in their work. Don't look at these as particular jobs in themselves but as skill sets which are valuable within any number of careers.

So avoid thinking about them too literally – the role of 'researcher' doesn't only play out in a lab or a library, and there are plenty of ways to be a 'teacher' without setting foot in a classroom. Resist stereotypes. Being a leader doesn't have to involve boardrooms and shouting. Not all creators carry paint brushes.

Your Starring Roles

Communicator	Analyser	Collaborator	Designer
writing; speaking; presenting; listening; interviewing; translating; performing; storytelling	*data analysis; critical thinking; fact checking; handling statistics*	*connecting people; building teams and partnerships; motivating others; mediating; negotiating*	*mapping out how something should be made, how a thing or system could look or work to be beautiful or functional*

Leader

managing people; setting goals and vision; strategic thinking; taking responsibility; influencing; guiding; decision-making

Organizer

planning and admin; coordinating people and tasks; managing projects; procuring goods or services; handling schedules and deadlines

Campaigner

empowering others; advocating; bringing about change; debating and building a persuasive case

Money Manager

budgeting; investing; fundraising; financing; auditing; accounting

Problem Solver

identifying challenges, risks or errors; generating alternatives; implementing fixes; developing action plans

Teacher

teaching; training; mentoring; coaching; facilitating; inspiring others; simplifying complex ideas

Creator

producing artistically or technically creative work; building something; getting your hands 'dirty'

Nurturer

providing emotional or practical support to other people or creatures; treating pain or need; healing

Innovator

inventing new products, services or ways of doing things; launching and developing; using entrepreneurial flair

Researcher

close reading; investigating; finding data; collating data, stories or information; writing reports; developing theories

Service Provider

identifying and meeting customers' needs; delivering great experiences; handling complaints; fixing problems

Seller

selling a product, service or idea; finding, attracting and persuading customers or clients; writing copy; negotiating deals

What we're interested in here is the activities that sit under particular roles and how you respond to them. Which would be your Starring Roles?

Using the blank chart below, consider each Starring Role and score your level of ability and your level of enjoyment out of ten, based on the scale given. You might like to note down any particular tasks you relish.

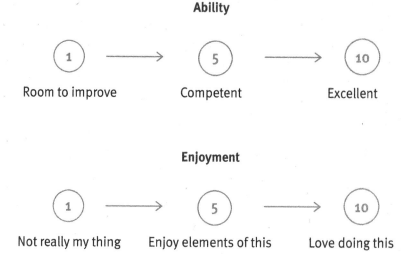

Ability

(1) ⟶ (5) ⟶ (10)

Room to improve   Competent   Excellent

Enjoyment

(1) ⟶ (5) ⟶ (10)

Not really my thing   Enjoy elements of this   Love doing this

Starring Roles

	Ability	Enjoyment	Favourite Tasks
Communicator			
Analyser			
Collaborator			
Designer			
Leader			

Organizer			
Campaigner			
Money Manager			
Problem Solver			
Teacher			
Creator			
Nurturer			
Innovator			
Researcher			
Service Provider			
Seller			

Now take a look at your scores.

- Where did you score highly on enjoyment but felt less sure about ability? How can you use that information? What are the possible implications of that?
- Where did you score highly on ability but were less enthusiastic? Have you taken a pathway where you are now an unfulfilled expert?
- Where are your sweet spots where you are both great at something and enjoy it too?
- If you had to choose just three Starring Roles, what would they be?
- Create a rough timetable for your perfect day or even week out of the many activities listed. How would you choose to spend your time? What would you spend the most time doing?

TIP: Go With the Flow

Tasks which fully capture your energy, focus and enjoyment and absorb you so much that you lose track of time are described as putting you into a state of 'flow'. The concept was developed by Hungarian–American psychologist Mihály Csíkszentmihályi, who set out to understand where in everyday life we feel really happy. His theory points to activities with the ideal combination of challenge, skill and creativity. Whether you call it flow or being in the zone, be on the lookout for these moments. 'Find out what you like and what you hate about life,' said Csíkszentmihályi. 'Start doing more of what you love, less of what you hate.' Just noticing how you feel whilst carrying out everyday tasks is a great place to start, whether you're organizing your wardrobe, researching your holiday or building a work presentation.

These exercises aren't just designed to identify what you're good at but also to help you prioritize the activities you want to form the backbone of your work.

Fiona, a graphic designer, had this realization about her current role:

'My favourite type of activity at work was always making the mock-ups, the brochures and books and physical point-of-sale pieces, actually physically making those. So after many years of sitting at a computer, learning software, I started to get a bit disheartened. I do like the creative side of the graphics, it's just sitting at the computer that I don't particularly enjoy. I did a graphic design degree and when I was at university, pretty much all of the work was done by hand, cutting out the type, the page layouts, and we had a small amount of work on a computer, very tiny Macs. And that's what I liked, making with my hands. But then I started to work in a design agency and so much of the work was all computer-based.'

The realization that she needed to get back to hands-on creativity was part of what led Fiona to train as a stone carver and start a portfolio career. You can read more about her journey on page 295.

Armed with the personal insights you've just created, look to the future:

Looking Ahead

What do I want to
do more of?

What do I want to
do less of?

What energizes me?

What drains me?

Now Write Your Own Reference

Taking what you've discovered about your Strengths and Skills and the activities you want to focus on in your future career, write your own reference for that ideal job. Don't worry that you don't know exactly what it is yet, just polish that skill set into a glowing description of all that you bring to your daily work. Set a timer for 5 minutes and try writing yourself a reference. If you find it helpful, use some of the prompts below.

Sally is an exceptional . . .
In a team, she brings . . .
She can always be relied upon to . . .
Her insight into . . .
She demonstrates excellent . . .
She shows . . .
As a manager/colleague, she . . .
Colleagues value her . . .

Why try it this way?

'When you use the third person, it's like you're tricking your protective, censoring ego into thinking you're writing about somebody else . . . writing in the third person, you're able to see a larger narrative of your life.'

Kim Schneiderman, Psychotherapist

STRENGTHS CASE STUDY

Chris

How playing to your strengths impacts your enjoyment of work:

In a decade working in the charity sector, Chris had gone from volunteer to Chief Executive Officer. The trouble was, he wasn't quite sure how. At 32, he felt like his career had happened to him more by accident than by design.

> 'At first I thought how lucky I was to have ended up here without ever having had a plan. But actually, I've realized that my accomplishments are down to having been in the right place at the right time, and often in situations where I didn't really feel like I belonged. I feel I've just made the best of the cards that fell into my lap and wonder what other paths I could have taken.'

A stint of volunteering overseas had turned into a role that was weighing Chris down.

> 'The word "leader" stresses me out. I don't want to have to be visionary and charismatic. It drains me to have to "perform" to trustees and be uplifting and inspiring. I want to get on with making projects happen, doing the practical stuff, not spending hours talking about the huge vision for ten years away.'

The strengths that Chris was having to call on in his role were not those that energized him. In fact, the opposite was true. As someone driven by excellence and achievement, constantly pulling on strengths that didn't come naturally was knocking his confidence and creating a sense of imposter syndrome. He came to me feeling inauthentic in his role and keen to explore a shift.

Chris's investigation of his strengths led him firmly to his pragmatism. He realized he took huge enjoyment from data analysis, problem-solving, people development and research to support far more immediate operations and targets. Strengths that he'd rather had to leave behind when he stepped up to the CEO role and became the lead actor rather than the stage manager.

He decided it made perfect sense for him to start looking at Chief Operating Officer roles instead, where he would retain the intellectual challenge, independence and seniority he wanted without being the face of an organization, with all that entailed. Chris turned to his additional interests in the environment, diversity and inclusion, and the museum sector to start his search.

Chris's case is a typical example of a career path that evolves in a direction that doesn't necessarily suit us, almost without us noticing. The classic case is the teacher who becomes a head and finds they are no longer teaching at all. You'll find another example of a career changer who found themselves promoted away from the skills they really enjoyed using in Dave's story on page 262.

Key Takeaways

It's easy to undervalue Strengths and Skills that come naturally to us.

You already know a great deal about yourself and your preferences, based on the life you've lived so far – making time to explore this is crucial.

Seeing ourselves through other people's eyes can be enlightening.

Being clear on what you are good at not only helps you decide what you want to do more of, it also builds your confidence in highlighting your expertise and abilities. Get in the habit of talking to your support team about your achievements and talents.

Being good at something is only part of the picture. The sweet spot is where what you are good at and what you enjoy cross over.

Action Checklist

- [ ] Personality Profile
- [ ] Unearth Your Strengths
- [ ] The Other Yous
- [ ] Playing with Perspectives
- [ ] Do They See What You See?
- [ ] Starring Roles
- [ ] Looking Ahead
- [ ] Write Your Own Reference

Before You Move On

Fill in the Strengths and Skills section on your Career Profile, paying particular attention to your favourite ones.

Chapter 4
What's Important to You

You should now be much clearer on your Strengths and Skills, particularly the ones you really want to draw on. But that's only one piece of the puzzle.

It's all very well being a great communicator, but if you're a vegan using those skills to sell beefburgers, it's no wonder something feels off.

You may be baffled as to why your analytical expertise as a barrister doesn't have you excited to dust off your wig after a long career break and skip back into court. Instead, you're demoralized by a sense that there's no room there for personal expression or growth.

Just because you're a brilliant computer scientist doesn't mean you'll work *anywhere* with the latest AI opportunities. If you feel you're not making the impact you want or finding the opportunities for collaboration you crave, your own skill set soon loses some of its appeal.

What's going on when you meet this kind of resistance? What's creating the disconnect between your abilities and what appears like an obvious career match? Say hello to your Work Values.

In this chapter, we're going deeper to find out what's really important to you about work. What motivates you and contributes to your all-important sense of purpose.

You may (or may not) *have* to work, but why do you *want* to work? What's going to make it as fulfilling and meaningful as possible? What will success look like for you?

Let's have a good rummage in your Why to help guide you towards your What.

What Are Values?

Values can be described as the core principles or fundamental beliefs by which you live your life. Interestingly, the word 'core' is thought to stem from the Latin word for heart. So we're connecting to something pretty deep-seated. Values are what's truly important to you and they're important to this journey because they have a strong bearing on how you choose to behave, what motivates the direction you take and shapes the decisions you make.

Some values feel pretty universal to the human existence: think of words like love, peace, honesty and justice. Those virtuous values you see carved around statue plinths or in gilded letters over historical institutions. These are essentially moral values, guiding us in issues of right and wrong. Many of these values are embedded in our childhood, via the influence of adults, family, school and wider society. They are less a personal choice and more an innate acceptance of a benevolent compass which keeps us all on (broadly!) the right track for a fair and happy society. Very few people would argue with these values or decide they'd like a different set: 'No love for me, thanks! And while we're at it, I utterly despise justice!'

So those are a given and not what we're after here. What we are interested in are your own personal values, specifically those associated with your work. Because this is where we all start to differ. Where our values become far more individual and therefore much more helpful to you in weighing up your options and guiding your decisions.

The process of identifying your values needs to be approached with a massive dose of authenticity and honesty. That can be both liberating and unsettling. You may worry that some values feel more impressive or worthy than others. Don't feel bad choosing 'Fun' over 'Helping Others'. Or owning the fact that 'Money' is important to you. I've lost count of the time people caveat their sentences to me with 'I know this sounds a bit shallow, but I think "Status" is important to me . . .' Or the opposite. 'I know I ought to be interested in "Excellence", but "Balance" is far more significant these days.'

Forget what looks good, what you 'ought' to value or what you think other people would expect you to say. How is that helpful in moving you forwards? For this process to work, you need to be honest with yourself. You may even find yourself wanting to reject work values you previously embraced, as you realize that they aren't really your values at all. They may be career values your parents or teachers instilled in you, or that seeped in during your time in a specific industry or sector, or even that you inadvertently adopted from a particular boss or team you worked with. And now they feel, well, 'off'.

It's worth noting that our Work Values can change over time. One reason that you may feel a strong need to reconsider your career after you've become a parent, as you hit mid-life or even after a global pandemic is that what feels important to you has shifted. You may now have more space to allow your Values to come into play. When you were right at the beginning of your career, the most pressing need may have been to find gainful employment after your studies, to move to a particular location, to pay your rent or to allow you to start saving for a deposit for a house.

If some of those practical elements of your life are now more or less under control, that may be why you're ready to go a bit deeper in considering what your work is really for.

How to Identify Your Work Values

It's tempting to see this a bit like a shopping expedition. I give you a list of Values and you bundle up the tastiest ones into your trolley until it's nearly overflowing. But this is not *Supermarket Sweep*. You're after quality and not quantity. You are looking for words that really resonate, that feel particularly meaningful and motivating. Not your nice-to-haves but your must-haves when you imagine any kind of future work. So ask yourself how bothered you would really be if you didn't get X or Y? Be brutal. If the lack of something doesn't concern you, or you're happy to pick it up in another area of your life instead, it isn't one of your core Work Values.

I've roughly grouped Values which could be considered related, but feel free to play around. Start by seeing which groups of words you are instinctively drawn to when you think about what's truly important to you about work.

Then consider each word in your favourite clusters. Look at the nuances of each one carefully and be curious about what it conjures up for you. Discard any that don't really capture what you're after.

You are aiming to settle on five key values that encompass what is truly important in your work. Feel free to choose your own words if they better capture what you're after.

Your Work Values

Adventure	Autonomy	Balance	Boldness
Fun	Freedom	Calmness	Challenge
Humour	Independence	Peace	Competition
Passion	Control	Simplicity	Risk
Recognition	Power	Predictability	Mastery
Respect	Influence	Security	Intellectual Rigour
Credibility	Leadership	Tradition	Expertise
Status	Authority	Routine	Wisdom
Organization	Learning	Variety	Helping Others
Practicality	Development	Novelty	Contribution
Efficiency	Self-improvement	Innovation	Service
Quality	Growth	Originality	Generosity
Achievement	Impact	Acquisition	Empowerment
Excellence	Inspiration	Abundance	Justice
Winning	Legacy	Comfort	Diversity
Perfection	Change	Money	Tolerance
Curiosity	Collaboration	Loyalty	Communication
Creativity	Community	Dependability	Connection
Imagination	Partnership	Trust	Improvement
Beauty	Teamwork	Support	Education

Just What Do You Mean?

A list of five words is all very well, but what do they symbolize for you? The pesky thing about Values is that they can feel a bit abstract. Do you want to know one of the most common things my clients say to me? 'I want my work to make an impact.' Which sounds marvellous. But what does impact actually look like? There's a whole spectrum to most of these Values – where are you aiming? Is impact hitting your monthly sales targets, helping one individual, fighting injustice, bringing about world peace?! There's no right definition here, only your definition.

Because what I mean by a particular value and what you mean may be two totally different things.

Take Creativity for example. Here's what Anna said:

'Creativity is about the freedom to think and act for myself. I can approach a problem in the way I want and I'm not micromanaged.'

Compare that to John's definition:

'Creativity is working with designs, colours and ideas. I can channel my imagination into something visual and beautiful, but also practical.'

Hmmm. See what I mean? Time to get specific and personal. Take your top five Values and write a short description to capture exactly what it is that's meaningful and important to you about them. You might want to use some of the other words from the cluster to help you.

Value	Description

Now you have your list of five and some juicy definitions, take a moment. Does that list feel like a true reflection of what motivates you? It should. Work that meets your Values will get you out of bed in the morning, even if it's not always perfect. It will be work that feels valuable and where you feel valued.

As we saw with your Strengths and Skills, it can be very helpful to tie your emerging self-knowledge to real-life experiences as a way of properly sense-checking what you're discovering.

Putting Your Values into Action

Finally, let's use your current and past experiences – both professional and personal – to see when you feel you have really been honouring your Values and felt more fulfilled as a result. Or where you have struggled to find your Values met.

Look back over previous jobs, friendships, voluntary activities and hobbies through these three lenses to see what lessons there are for you going forwards with your career redesign.

Action

What kind of activities
allow you to live out your
Values? What activities
challenge your Values?

People

Where do you find people
who share your Values?
Where have you found
your Values at odds with
others?

Environment

What kind of places,
organizations, industries
or sectors align with your
Values? Which feel
unconnected?

VALUES CASE STUDY

Erica

How values can help you better understand yourself and what drives you forward

Erica had been working as Head of Internal Communications at a large utilities firm for 30 years and – at 51 – was facing redundancy as her company was winding down.

When we first met, it was clear that the upheaval that was to come had Erica fluctuating between stomach-squeezing fear and a sense of exciting new opportunity. Here was a moment of possible reinvention – but was it 'a massive void in front of me' or 'some kind of positive future that I can take control of'?

Erica was clear that as a self-confessed 'Steady Eddie' she would probably have stayed put until retirement if her hand hadn't been forced. 'I never really knew what I wanted to do when I grew up – and just fell into a job where I have stayed.' There was a welcome sense of security and predictability in her current job.

But as she described her 30 years as a 'great grey blob' with very few highlights, she became increasingly aware that – whilst the job had worked on a practical level for her family and she'd enjoyed the company of some great colleagues – it had long ago stopped feeling meaningful. 'I'm simply hiding, but fundamentally I know I need to do something. Now I have a chance to rock my boat . . . and I want to see where it takes me.'

When Erica dug into her values, there were huge clues as to why she'd stayed with one company so long, but why she also had misgivings about the nature of the work she was in.

Safety

Peace Of Mind

Honesty

Fairness

Belonging

'I got cosy,' said Erica, which was borne out by her values of Safety, Peace of Mind and Belonging. But what about Fairness and Honesty? She wasn't convinced about a role that she saw as essentially communicating a company line.

'I feel what I do doesn't make any real difference to people. My late husband was a headteacher for many years and I always admire the impact he had on real people's lives.'

Even though it would mean stepping out of her comfort zone, it became clear to her that staying within the utilities sector wasn't going to cut it. We discussed strategies to help her continue to feel 'safe' whilst taking more risks with her future.

During our work together, Erica realized that her values of Fairness and Honesty were crucial to her future. She realized they already showed up powerfully in her voluntary roles as a school governor and trustee, where she felt she could make a meaningful impact on creating a level playing field for young people in education. She enjoyed asking challenging questions of those in power to bring about change.

Guided by her values, Erica has taken a job in a charity where she will 'actually be making things better and creating a more equitable society'.

Defining Success

Time to play with another important idea when it comes to your work satisfaction: Success.

Getting clear on the outcome you're looking for before you start can have a huge bearing on the pathway you choose. And once again, it requires some radical honesty, whether you're going full pelt towards a six-figure salary and luxury holidays, being a role model for your kids or bringing about change in your local community.

Defining what Success means to you should be a judgement-free zone. That may mean shaking off other people's expectations or overriding the inner voice telling you what you 'should' be aiming for. Setting coordinates for a place you don't really want to go will end in a pretty miserable journey.

Let's start by exploring your assumptions and reactions to the whole concept of Success.

Write a few lines in response to these questions:

- What do I picture when I hear someone described as having 'a hugely successful career'? To what extent does this feel like a helpful definition of success for me?
- Which elements of traditional success do I want to embrace?

- Which elements do I wish to redefine?

Now let's get specific and build your own version of Success.

Success generally fixates on a fairly narrow definition of what you achieve in life. It has something of an external quality – focused on what you gain or achieve. Things outside of yourself. It's common to think of success as a pinnacle that you want to reach, meaning you need to strive until you arrive at a certain height. And that once you are there you ought to be totally satisfied.

Rather than thinking of Success as an end goal to achieve, it can be far more interesting to consider success as a more rounded state of being in which you want to operate. You can try this using the BE–DO–HAVE exercise below, which invites you to try breaking down what you want or need to feel successful into three components, only one of which is about what you HAVE. And even that might not be in the obvious material sense.

Write down the answers to the following three questions. I've set out an example on page 87 to help you.

BE

What kind of person do I want to be?

If you're going old-school, then rich and famous may well make an appearance here. But I'd invite you to think about your whole life as well as your professional world and find all the things you would BE if you were a success on your own terms. They might be adjectives which detail your mental or physical state, such as relaxed, balanced, calm, dynamic, healthy, grateful and so on. They might be short descriptions, like a great dad, a thought leader, an inspiration to others, a role model or a changemaker.

An interesting way to do this is to play with perspectives and think about how you'd like other people to describe you. If you fancy a quirky detour for some extra inspiration at this stage, try writing your own one paragraph obituary and think how you'd like your work, your attitude and your contribution to be remembered by your work colleagues.

DO

What will I be doing when I feel successful?

Think about what you would need to actively DO to be the person you just described.

Don't worry, I'm not talking specifically here about the job you'll be doing. We're not quite there yet. This column is where you can focus on the habits and activities that contribute to making you feel successful, whether those are holistic (eating healthily, exercising twice a week, travelling, seeing friends) or in your work (learning new things all the time, serving the next generation, making an impact on the world, demonstrating excellence).

I'd suggest you look back at the Work Values you identified earlier on pages 79–81 and consider how you could bring those to life in the things you DO. Write down what you realize. If Adventure is one of your values, what will you need to be doing to successfully meet that value? If Creativity is something you aspire to, how will that positively manifest itself in your activities?

HAVE

What will I have in order to feel successful?

Traditionally, success has required some pretty hefty material things in the HAVE column. But as you'll see from my examples, this needn't be all about possessions.

If you desperately want a new car, a leadership position or a six-month trip around the world, you should absolutely feel free to put that in your HAVE column. This is *your* definition.

But think of the less tangible measures you put on your

success too. This might include having strong relationships (a successful marriage, deep friendships), having certain feelings or experiences (security, autonomy) or having a particular legacy to leave after you are gone, whether that is happy children or a fairer workplace.

What Does Success Mean to You

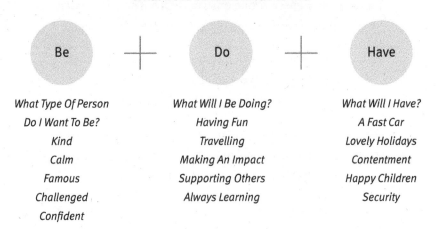

What Type Of Person Do I Want To Be?	What Will I Be Doing?	What Will I Have?
Kind	Having Fun	A Fast Car
Calm	Travelling	Lovely Holidays
Famous	Making An Impact	Contentment
Challenged	Supporting Others	Happy Children
Confident	Always Learning	Security

Use your answers to write your own definition of success in one paragraph:

Key Takeaways

Getting clear on your Work Values will help you understand what your career means to you at a deeper level. It will allow you to engage with your purpose and what you need for your work to fulfil your needs.

There are no right or wrong answers when it comes to what you want from work. Being honest is vital to this process.

Success is a concept which comes with a lot of baggage. Being curious about how you personally define career success should help you feel happier in your life.

Consider that success is not a pinnacle to be reached but a consistent state in which you are able to be, do and have what feels authentic and important.

Action Checklist

☐ Your Work Values

☐ Just What Do You Mean?

☐ Putting Your Values into Action

☐ Defining Success

Before You Move On

Fill in your Work Values and your Definition of Success on your Career Profile.

Chapter 5
How You Want to Work

I've noticed that many of my clients have a clear sense of the way they want to work long before they know what they'd actually like to be doing.

Take Hannah – in our first session together, the 36-year-old office manager talked me through some of the things she'd achieved to date. My ears pricked up when she said she'd trained as a yoga teacher and had run some online classes. As a friend, I would probably have leapt on that – 'Why not set up your own yoga studio? A no-brainer surely? I can see it now! Yes, do it! You could *so* do that!' As a friend, I would have heard her problem (*I don't know what I want to do*) and I would have wanted to dive in and fix it (*here's the obvious idea*). As a coach, I kept my mouth shut and kept listening.

Because it soon became clear that Hannah didn't want to set up her own business. In fact, she was dead set on *not* doing that. Yes, she had the skills and the interest in yoga. But working alone as an entrepreneur was something that held absolutely no appeal.

As you're hopefully starting to see, this is a puzzle with lots of different pieces and they all need to fit together in a way that feels balanced and meaningful for you.

So in this chapter, we'll investigate your ideal working environment – the kind of people around you, the shape of your week, the type of company, the structure of the organization, thoughts about employment versus going it alone . . .

We'll also pause here to check in on what this information may have to tell you about how radical a change you want to make. Because when you get curious about what does and doesn't work for you, there can be intriguing realizations about whether some strategic changes to your existing role or profession might (or might not!) be enough to make you feel fulfilled.

Where? Who? How?

I want you to spend some time picturing your ideal work environment. You're not looking here for the actual job you're doing but a sense of *where* you're doing it, *who* you're doing it with and *how* you're doing it. As you make notes in response to the following prompts, allow your mind to reach more clearly for the images that always float in the background when you daydream about your new career. Write down any significant preferences and realizations. This is definitely a three brains kind of exercise, with your heart and your gut playing a big role alongside your head. When your head kicks in, notice if it offers you reservations or resistance, and be curious about what that's telling you.

Think About Where

When you picture your ideal work environment, where do you naturally see yourself?

Type

Organizations and employers come in all shapes and sizes. Are you drawn to a large, medium or small organization? Are you more inclined towards the private sector or the public sector? Do charity or not-for-profit bodies feel like a good fit? Would you love to be part of a big name, an established organization with immediate brand recognition, or could you see yourself getting stuck in at a scrappy start-up?

Culture

Consider the feel of this imaginary place. Are you hankering for the corporate world and visualizing yourself in a sharp suit or does a dress code, spoken or unspoken, fill you with horror? Are you more comfortable with traditional or unconventional approaches? Do you thrive in a buzzy, fast-paced, challenging environment or prefer a calmer, steadier atmosphere? What about the structure – do you favour a clear hierarchy with defined roles and an obvious pecking order, or is a flatter structure with fewer levels of management more appealing? What values does this workplace demonstrate?

Location

Is the physical location of your work significant to you? At its simplest, this could involve thinking about whether you work from home, go into an office or use a co-working space – or some kind of hybrid model. Do you see yourself in your local neighbourhood, somewhere rural or heading into a city centre? Or would you like to ditch the indoors and mostly work outside?

On a practical level, do you have views on how long you're prepared to commute if needed? Do you have a specific target location? Would you actively welcome the chance for some travel, and if so, are you picturing yourself on train journeys around the country or flights overseas? Does working away from home mean international conferences, in-depth research trips, fieldwork of some kind, or client and site visits? Is this happening every week or twice a year?

INSIGHT

Can *How* You Work Be More Important than *What You Earn*?
Playing with the relative importance of all the elements of your ideal work is a very personal process. The weight you give to different pieces of the puzzle will ultimately depend on your own circumstances, values and *desired outcome*.

I had a fascinating conversation with Amy, a digital marketer, who ended up co-founding her own company. She told me how she had turned down a great corporate job with a big salary because it didn't match the promises she had made herself about how she wanted to work.

'Because of where it was and the long hours that would be involved, I realized that job would never allow me to do the two things I had identified as massively important to my overall happiness and wellbeing – to be able to cycle to work and to own a dog.' By setting up her own agency, Amy compromised on income to enable her to have an office near her home, the freedom to control her own hours and even bring her dog to work when she needed to.

Think About Who

In this future career universe, what are you doing in relation to other people? Who are the people around you and how would you define those relationships?

You

Are you imagining yourself in a leadership role, managing people? If so, are you overseeing a small team, a department or the whole company? Or are you part of the team, working in a group either big or small? Do you work closely on ideas and projects or only come together for meetings to share updates on your own individual part of the operation? Is your boss hands-on or hands-off? Perhaps other people barely feature, because you see yourself mostly working alone rather than on group projects?

Colleagues

If you see yourself with colleagues, what do you love about them? Are they like you in age, outlook, background and experience, or a more diverse bunch? Are these purely professional relationships confined to the office or do you want teammates who socialize and even become friends? Do you want them to share your values and feel like kindred spirits or bring totally different perspectives to the table?

Clients/Customers

If you have customers or clients, what characterizes them? What kind of people do you enjoy working for or helping? How do they treat you?

Think About How

Keep visualizing that – for now – imaginary career. Many types of work can be done in totally different ways. So how do you see yourself working?

Employed

Consider how strongly you gravitate towards a traditional way of working. Employment means a regular salary, an agreed working pattern, paid holidays, benefits such as maternity leave, sick pay, a pension scheme and someone else thinking about your taxes. It also means someone else is in charge. Does this feel safe and secure or restrictive?

Remember there are many different forms of employment to think about. What would be your ideal working hours? Do you like a set pattern or shift work? Would you like to work full-time or part-time? Could you look at compressed hours or flexitime? Don't overlook innovative options like a job share or finite chunks of work like a maternity cover or fixed-term contracts.

Self-employed

Have you thought of working as a freelancer, consultant or contractor? As your own boss, you could have more control over your work schedule. You can take on the projects you really enjoy and say no to those you don't, and create variety by working with several different clients at the same time.

But of course *you've* got to find those clients! Unless you hire help, you'll be doing your own admin and accounts. You won't qualify for perks like holiday or sick pay and your income is not guaranteed. You may relish going it alone or worry about the lack of other people and support. Mind you, you needn't be totally solo. You can be self-employed but form some kind of partnership or become one of a team of freelancers taking on work outsourced by a bigger firm.

Entrepreneur

It's another form of self-employment but setting up and running your own business somehow feels like a step up. How do you respond to the words entrepreneur, founder or business owner?

For some people, building their own thing is the ultimate in creativity, freedom and satisfaction. They see an opportunity to generate a bigger income, pursue a genuine passion or make an impact no one else has made. All of which can happen.

Are you big on drive and self-motivation? Happy to do all the mundane tasks as well as come up with the big ideas? You may need to raise money or invest your own, which carries an element of risk. It can be challenging to establish healthy boundaries between work and life when you are getting something off the ground. Would you have support from your family and friends?

Portfolio Career

Before you fall into thinking you need to jump in just one direction, what about combining multiple streams of income in a portfolio career? Perhaps you could be employed as an accountant three days a week and teach private French lessons on the other two. Or work freelance as a graphic designer for two days a week and work in-house at a big marketing company on the others.

A portfolio career can be a short-term approach or a permanent solution and can serve many purposes. It can allow you to combine something more traditional with something more creative. It can marry a steady source of income with a less predictable one. Allow you to keep paying the bills whilst developing a new project. Play to different periods of the year when demand for certain work fluctuates. Combine paid and voluntary work. Or perhaps it will simply take into account your love of variety in your work.

What's right for you is very personal. Consider these two contrasting views.

Sarah made a move from being employed as a veterinary nurse to running her own business as a soft tissue therapist:

> 'It's the best, best thing that I've ever done because it's my business, my rules. I fit it around family, I don't have to answer to anyone. I'm really passionate about what I do, so I like things done well and I want them done properly, and it really irritates me if they aren't. So I know that what I do, it's done to the best of my ability, and that's what I try and strive for in my business.'

In contrast, Victoria is training as a nurse after twenty years freelancing in the publishing industry:

> 'A couple of years ago I was so daunted by the next twenty years, thinking, am I going to be freelance all my life? Now having experienced working life in a hospital, I can't compare this to my previous working life. It's exciting in the hospital. I get to work with all kinds of talented and highly skilled people instead of being on my own editing books. And you learn how to deal with feedback. That's all part of building your confidence, you know, and it's very hard to do that in isolation.'

You'll find Sarah and Victoria's full stories and reflections on different ways of working from other people who've made a switch in Chapter 12. Take a look at Katherine, Janette and Sarah's thoughts if you're thinking of going it alone.

Paint That Future

When you've answered these questions, consider how strongly you feel about each area. If you were scratching about for an answer at any point, it may be that you feel pretty flexible about certain things and are open to a number of possibilities. That's fine.

But we definitely want to capture any powerful preferences, strong images or surges of excitement and create a real vision of the work environment you are aiming for. What you know you don't want can loom quite large, especially if you have been unhappy in previous roles. If that happens, try to flip the coin. Rather than saying, 'I don't want to feel unsupported by my manager,' identify what you do want instead, for example: 'I have a manager who meets with me regularly to listen and collaborate, agreeing clear and measurable outcomes.'

Shape your notes into a one-page description of your ideal work set-up. Your mind is capable of painting one hell of a picture! You can add in the core skills you see yourself using, based on the work you did in Chapter 3. You might not know exactly what work you are doing but you know the kind of activities that would fill your ideal day. So paint yourself a vision of your future work featuring your How, your Where, your Who and your What with as much energy and detail as you can.

Here's an example adapted from a real client.

> Where I work is flexible. There is an official site, but I get to work in different places and from home when I want. I spend time in the countryside / nature / outdoors and in a city / cities with access to modern culture. I have flexible working hours.
>
> There is a culture of mutual respect. We don't need to

clock-watch or worry what others are doing because we know and trust everyone is pulling their weight. We are outcome-focused; we know the purpose of what we're doing and will get the job done well over caring how we get there. There is a culture of ownership and accountability. People don't blame others or make excuses when they mess up, they just get on with it.

The culture is fast-paced and demanding. There's always a buzz of lots of important things happening. People expect and can depend on hard work, excellence and a can-do attitude from everyone. There is a culture of innovation and breaking down barriers, etc. Everyone feels challenged and able to learn and grow but not unreasonably stressed or out of their depth. Everyone feels comfortable to ask for help or say when they don't know something without fear of criticism.

The company / organization is pretty big and has professional operations in place. We don't have to waste time fixing the printer! It is not pretentious or stuffy, but it is professional. People aren't scruffy or lazy. People want to work with us and be involved. We offer something they want and need and that brings something good to the world.

The leadership are credible, inspiring, have integrity, are respectful and show recognition of everyone but are not overly soft, don't micromanage and spend their time well. They are clear about what they expect, make sure we have what we need to do our jobs well and ensure there are opportunities for progression.

I'm part of a peer team who collaborate, knowing what each other is working on and bouncing ideas off each other, but will mainly work autonomously and have their own areas of specialism / focus. They are intelligent, fun, hard-working, positive, up for a challenge, constructively critical, and have a useful, fresh perspective. I respect them and can learn from them, and vice versa.

My work is varied, some desk-based, some out and about. I meet with people to research, analyse and share information. I am a problem solver, busy with the planning and implementation of new projects and ideas. I use my creative skills to present my work and produce documents, simplifying complex concepts and coming up with innovative approaches. I am a brilliant organizer and enjoy mentoring younger colleagues.

I look forward to each day and each day brings something new.

TIP: How Do You Visualize Your Future?

I'm asking you to commit a lot of your thoughts and ideas to paper. It's a great way of processing, prioritizing and sorting through what's in your head and describing your desired career in real terms. But if you find writing in this way challenging, perhaps you are more of a visual thinker. You might try summarizing your ideal future as a mind map (see page 129). Or consider doing this exercise as a Pinterest board instead, or create a vision board using images and words cut out from old newspapers and magazines. The aim is to build a collage which embodies all the thoughts you have around your ideal working life – whether that is pictures, quotes, odd words or snippets of an article.

When you've painted your future, it's time to assess how close this vision is to your current reality.

Now is a great moment to pause and anchor these thoughts to

your current or previous work to see how far off you have been and what valuable lessons or patterns you can find.

When you break your work down into these different components, it's much easier to spot any pain or pleasure points, often recurring ones that you keep inadvertently getting wrong! It's too easy to say 'I hated that job' or 'that role was really boring' without getting curious or specific enough about what wasn't doing it for you.

Was it *where* you were working? *How* you were working? The *people* alongside you? Or *what* you were doing?

Sometimes, an on-paper-perfect job can be ruined by an overly demanding boss or marred by the lack of like-minded colleagues. So it's not *what* you're doing that's the real problem but *who* you're doing it with. Conversely, a fabulously fun team may not be enough to make up for the long hours and travel requirements of your work – the *how* simply can't be overridden by the *who*.

It's worth looking for the areas which feel most important to you as that may dictate where you focus your attention and where you are happy to compromise. For you, it may be that the right colleagues are everything and trump the sector or organization you're in every time – your *who* will always outweigh your *where*. Or you might be prepared to fill the photocopier and make the coffee if it means being part of the business of your dreams – in which case your *what* is far less of a big deal than your *where*.

Using the table opposite, list all your jobs to date. Then fill in the columns, noting down the elements which did or didn't work for you. For each area, give yourself a score on a scale of 1 to 10, where 1 is a very poor match to your ideal set-up and left you highly dissatisfied and 10 is a fantastic match and meant that element was really fulfilling. What do you notice?

Where? How? Who? What?

Job	Where	How	Who	What
	Location *The* *organization* *Its culture*	*Working* *patterns* *Nature of your* *employment*	*Your status* *Your colleagues* *Your clients*	*Mix of activities* *Use of your* *skills*
	/10	/10	/10	/10

INSIGHT

Chop or Change?

This practical focus on your career environment can feel rather mundane compared to the last chapter's deep work of discovering the real purpose of your work. Nonetheless, it has the same aim – to help you develop some guiding principles for your next steps, enabling you to both course-correct and to recreate any elements that really work for you.

It may surprise you to know that not all thoughts of a career change end in a hugely radical overhaul. You don't always want to throw the baby out with the bathwater. There are a range of reasons for wanting to shift careers and not all of them are as enormous as you might first think. Whilst the 'biggies' certainly involve a burning desire to develop a totally different skill set and take up a whole new mission in life, it's fair to say that many people's dissatisfaction comes from an underlying unhappiness caused by stress, a lack of work-life balance, uninspiring surroundings, a toxic culture or a feeling that their presence is neither impactful nor rewarded.

That may be tackled by the full 'chop' – ditching your role for something completely different – or by implementing 'change' – identifying the parts of the puzzle that no longer fit and taking steps to alter them.

What are you sensing so far about whether you are driven to give your career the full chop or to change certain elements of it informed by what you are discovering?

Two simple questions to reflect on at this stage:

— What would I need to change to make my work work for me?

— What is most out of kilter with what I want and need?

Stuart, whose Why you heard back in Chapter 2, was a miserable lawyer who became a fulfilled lawyer in his early thirties by making a change to where he worked. He shifted from media law, where he struggled to feel he was having any impact, to working for a philanthropic foundation. 'I was more or less at the stage of giving up on law because I didn't think I could be happy as a lawyer, but it turns out I just needed the right job and to work towards a cause that I care about.'

You can read more of Stuart's story on page 287.

Think About How Much

Just before we leave the practicalities of any future career, we should talk money. I'm giving the issue of earnings a separate section, because it's a big practical consideration, requiring a spot of budget investigation and it's also likely to force you back into the more philosophical territory we roamed around in the last chapter.

As you know from thinking about what motivates you, your attitude to money is very personal.

It may be weighing heavily on your mind as a potential barrier to change – 'I'd love to retrain but I just don't think I can afford a cut in salary with my rent and childcare costs. I'm the primary earner in my family.'

It may be of relatively little importance at all, perhaps because you find yourself with a degree of financial security – 'My partner is the main breadwinner, meaning I have a bit more flexibility in my choices' or 'I have a redundancy package that's bought me some time'.

Or it may not be something that will ever feel like a deciding factor – 'The money has never been important to me. As long as I can pay my rent, I'll make career choices based on other factors.'

Wherever you find yourself on that spectrum, you'll be dealing with the curious interplay between two financial factors – want and need.

So let me first ask you two simple questions. The answers themselves are important. The relationship between the two figures is where it gets interesting!

What Do You *Need* to Earn?

How clear are you on your finances? As you consider your career change, are you confident about how much room you have to manoeuvre? What you discover here may influence what decisions you make about investing in training, changing your hours, the kind of industry you move into and how long you want to take to make your career move.

So now is an important time to do a proper bit of budgeting and produce something quite specific.

If you're one of those people who knows almost to the pound how much is in their bank account, has a handle on their mortgage rate and the price of their latest gas bill, this won't take long. But if your finances are a hot mess, may I suggest now is a good moment to sit down with a calculator and a clear head.

At the most basic level, you'll want to get a good handle on your outgoings – key figures like your rent/mortgage, regular savings or pension contributions, your utility bills, phone and Wi-Fi, your grocery spend, childcare, running a car or travel costs and so on. Factor in your spending on things like gym memberships, holidays, Christmas and birthday gifts, going out and clothes. Grab your bank and credit card statements and household bills to build as accurate a picture as possible. Here are two resources to help you.

- Moneysavingexpert offers two downloadable spreadsheets, both Excel or Open Office, where you can detail all your income and outgoings: https://www.moneysavingexpert.com/banking/budget-planning/
- Citizens Advice Bureau have a 30-minute online budgeting tool to help you understand what you're earning and spending: https://www.citizensadvice.org.uk/debt-and-money/budgeting/budgeting/work-out-your-budget/budgeting-tool/

Arming yourself with this financial information could be important in deciding what options are open to you, what avenues you need to investigate or what conversations you need to have with a partner or yourself about household income, savings and long-term aspirations.

Dave, a hotel procurement contractor turned software developer, sat down with his wife and took this process seriously.

'We didn't have any savings, never had any kind of inheritance money or anything, and we've worked for everything we have. We do have quite a big mortgage and a nice house, which we obviously bought based on our earnings. So this career change period was always going to be a bit scary, but we just cut back on everything that wasn't necessary, and there was quite a lot when we looked at it. I think I was paying over £200 a month for my gym membership, which went straightaway, and things like TV subscriptions. We cut things back for myself and my wife but not the kids, they weren't impacted. And we were confident that this was just a stepping stone and that ultimately, in a couple of years' time, we would be fine again and hopefully in a better position. We did the maths and decided to take a hit, because you live your job so much and it really was affecting my mood at home. And we've managed to make it work.'

For Dave, his career change required a period of lower earnings before getting his salary back up. You can hear more from Dave on page 262. Later in the book we'll examine the assumption that a career change has to mean investing in expensive courses or taking a pay cut to start at the beginning.

What Do You *Want* to Earn?

Whilst money may not have been one of your final five Work Values, or even close, it's good to check in here anyway. Often I find unpredictable things can happen in this space.

Psychologists have a field day with money and our relationship with it. Money can symbolize so many different things: happiness, security, power, status, freedom, comfort. I wonder what it means to you.

Money may be a big motivator spurring you on to make a move and make your millions – 'My ideal job will allow me to retire in ten years' time and travel the world.' You don't need that much money, but you really want it.

Or you might be someone who doesn't want what you believe a fat paycheck represents. One client told me: 'I don't need a big salary if that comes with responsibility.'

Another felt the need not for a big salary but a fair one: 'Money isn't a key factor, as long as I'm getting the right market rate for the role that I am doing.'

Sometimes I work with people who find the need to earn a

major salary isn't essential for them. If you and your partner have lived predominantly on one salary over the years whilst you were the primary carer for your children, you may have become used to that situation. That's not to say it wasn't without its financial sacrifices, but it may mean there is no pressing *need* for a second salary.

But not *needing* a specific figure doesn't mean you don't *want* to earn a particular amount. That you'll work for peanuts or at a lower rate than you are qualified for.

So what is the figure you want to earn and how similar is it to the amount you need to earn?

And, crucially, what's the timescale here? What you need to earn may have an urgency to it. What you want to earn may require you to play a longer game.

As ever, there's no right answer. Just see what bubbles up and try to be as truthful with yourself as possible. Think about the implications of your career change on what you need to earn and what you want to earn. If you want to spend more time considering this, revisit the Go Below questions from Chapter 2.

Key Takeaways

There are many factors at play in any job and how contented we feel in it – the place, the people, the hours, the tasks, the money . . . Be on the lookout for which pieces of the puzzle feel most significant to you.

Noticing any particular pain or pleasure points from your previous or current work can be a powerful indicator of where change is needed.

Consider the concept of 'chop' or 'change'. How radical a move do you feel drawn to? What changes could you make now?

An assessment of your current spending and earning will help you work out accurately the salary you need to earn and could give you a better idea about the options open to you.

What you earn may be about more than simply the money.

Action Checklist

- [ ] Think About Who
- [ ] Think About Where
- [ ] Think About How
- [ ] Paint That Future
- [ ] Where? How? Who? What?
- [ ] Think About How Much

Before You Move On

Fill in the Ideal Work Environment section on your Career Profile.

Don't forget to include a note about your ideal salary.

Chapter 6

What Interests and Excites You

Do you feel wildly driven by a particular passion? Lucky you. Fantastic! We definitely want to investigate that. But for many of us, the suggestion to just 'follow your passion' is stressful, awkward and unhelpful. Hobbies? Pah. The idea of hobbies may have gone out the window with the birth of your first child. Many of us have seen our individual interests subsumed by family life or busy jobs, and it's become a struggle to find the time and energy to reconnect with what lights us up.

So in this chapter we're going to get creative. We'll spread the net wide and go looking for clues to capture your Interests – past, present and even virtual.

What you do with this information is going to be up to you. Could your Interests hold the key to your career change? It's another part of the puzzle and for some people it's directly related and crucial to their future work, for others less so. Just because you like cooking doesn't mean you should retrain as a pastry chef. An interest in politics shouldn't necessarily have you knocking on doors asking old ladies if you can count on their vote. Though it might.

After digging into your Interests, you are likely to find:

- Some interests are going to remain firmly in the hobby zone as a source of fun, stimulation and relaxation. And there's no shame in that.
- One or two interests may really grab you and make you wonder if you could take something you love and make it pay.
- Plenty of recurring interests and themes that you might want to factor into your thinking about where you work and what you do.

This chapter is not a simplistic attempt to find one burning passion and turn it into a profession. There's an unhelpful idea that's developed around passion-driven careers, that there is a small, elite band of people who make money doing only what they utterly adore, and then there's the rest of us – a bunch of dullards toiling away unfulfilled until we can find the one magic match to ignite our fervour. In reality, there's a much broader spectrum of how our interests and our work intersect and it's up to you where you'd like to park yourself.

Your Interests can form a rich source of data to help shape rather than rigidly dictate your career choices. We're looking to investigate patterns about what's really going on when you say you love space travel and fashion magazines, so you can deepen your self-knowledge and open up some new work possibilities but don't accidentally follow your 'passion' off a cliff if that's not really right for you.

7 Ways to Unearth Your Interests

1. Reading Between the Lines

If you had two minutes to grab a handful of magazines
before a long flight, what would you choose? Which books

would be first in your beach bag? If you had to subscribe to one magazine for a year and promise to read it religiously, what would you go for?

2. Supernatural Study

You are sent back to a fantasy school for a year, where students can study absolutely anything they want for fun or for expertise. What would your Fantasy Timetable look like? Choose at least three academic subjects and three practical ones. If you could wave a wand now and have one additional qualification (at any level!), what would it be?

3. Down the Rabbit Hole

What are your guilty online secrets? Where do you get lost on Instagram, Facebook or Twitter and find 10 minutes has become an hour because you were so engrossed?

4. Childhood Dreams

'And what do you want to do when you grow up?' Carefully revisit stages of your childhood up to the age of 18 . . . What did you love to do? What were you good at? Which were your favourite toys or games? What was the teenage dream you had for your adult self?

5. Access All Areas

You can have a coffee with the head of any organization, the designer of any product or the creator of any project, however big or small. Who would you want to meet and why? What would you talk to them about? Then you can spend a week exploring behind the scenes at any organizations or places you like. Where would you choose to go?

6. Tiger Parenting

Which hobbies do you find yourself encouraging in your children, if you have them? Which of their clubs and activities do you most enjoy hearing about or like to get involved with? What do you wish had been on offer when you were young?

7. Screentime

What documentaries or current affairs programmes do you like to watch on TV? Which shows transport you to a world you love? Which one do you dream of presenting or taking part in? What subject would you like to make a TV show about?

This a creative and fun exercise, exploring your current reality to see what that has to tell you, but also journeying back in time and even suspending reality to try a few new perspectives to fire up your imagination.

Remember Fiona who took her graphic design skills into stone carving? A few reflections on her childhood and what interested her underlined her need for hands-on creativity and a deep-seated love of natural materials:

'Both my dad and grandad were carpenters and as a child I liked hanging around their sheds . . . the smell and trying to make things in there. For a while when I was about 14 I thought about being an architect. And I remember a period when I went travelling during my twenties. While I was away, I was always looking at the buildings and surrounding nature – I spent a lot of time in Australia and saw so much open space, nature, rocks but also architecture. When I was in New York, there were people doing stone carving on a church, cutting the stone in situ. In Singapore, I saw men working on a building, doing a similar thing but in a completely different material, more of a clay, modelling shapes on to a building. And someone I met in a desert in Australia was carving things into talc and rocks. I even came back with a little collection of stones from different places!'

Victoria, who moved from publishing to nursing aged 47, would have done well to notice what she was reading and watching in the years before her career shift.

'When I worked in publishing, I oversaw lots of health books, particularly on the human body, because I'm a bit obsessed! I've always had a fascination, and I've watched countless TV documentaries on operations. So I guess the idea of nursing had been lying there, unconsciously. I'd always felt a bit odd reading medical books, but the first thing I did when I started nurse training was to listen to Bill Bryson's *The Body*, and I loved the fact that I could now legitimately listen to this book without feeling like a weirdo!'

There may be things staring you in the face in a similar way, but actually the real nuggets in these scenarios are not always obvious at first glance.

Let me explain . . .

Say you passionately wanted to be a hairdresser when you were eight. The outcome of this exercise is not to suggest you should now become a hairdresser. The key is to ask yourself *what* it was about hairdressing that appealed to you.

Was it the creativity? Working closely with customers? Running your own business? Following the latest fashions?

Or let's suppose you find yourself heavily involved in your daughter's football club.

Should you qualify as a sports coach? Not necessarily. But what is that telling you about yourself? Is it an interest in fitness and well-being? Or more about the love of the team dynamic, regardless of the context? Perhaps the leadership involved in pulling together a bunch of people to achieve a goal? The satisfaction of planning and delivering a training programme?

Don't feel the pressure to find a grand passion, though if you already have one or hit on one, feel free to grab it. Rather, dig deeper to unearth what your Interests say about you. Often we are told if we just follow our passion, career satisfaction will follow. But we don't all have one overriding passion, or the luxury of pursuing it if we do.

So go over your answers looking for clues and repeating patterns, and think beyond the obvious. It's important here to use some of the Curiosity techniques outlined in Chapter 2. This is definitely a time to 'Go Below' and get 'Pattern Spotting'. And you should really 'Follow the Energy'. What feels compelling and exciting?

TIP: Not Everything is About Work

You'll soon realize that some interests you have could be termed 'passive' and some are much more 'active'. There's a big difference between enjoying 'going to the theatre' when a friend invites you and being the person who's first online to book every new West End show. Between 'liking nature' and going wild camping every other weekend. That's not to diminish your interests. You don't have to be a total zealot. But now is the time to think about which are happy hobbies and which might have something to say to you about your career choices.

This is absolutely a time to 'Think Whole Life' – my clients often notice at this stage that there are activities they really enjoy that they've lost sight of and would like to reconnect with. Not necessarily as a new career path but just as a way of creating more balance in their life and building a richer experience overall. If that's you, take some time to work out how you'd like to incorporate those old hobbies back into your world.

As you reflect on what you've written, start capturing anything that feels significant in the Emerging Ideas chart overleaf. Whilst the nominal focus of this chapter has been your Interests, I hope you've seen that there's much more to how you spend your time than a random selection of activities. In a lovely bit of emerging symmetry, you'll probably find some overlap with the work you've already done on what you are good at, what's important to you and the environment you'd like to work in. Get stuck in. Let me take this moment to encourage you to keep writing things down and not be tempted to just think. Capturing your thoughts in this way allows you to return to them more than once and more easily notice patterns and significant words.

This exercise should feel fun, exciting and expansive. It's shifting you into the realms of possibility, freeing you from the constraints of normal life and inviting you to get curious about what this means for your future.

We're coming to the end of Step Two – Reflecting – and there should be a much clearer image in front of you of who you really are and how you want that to guide your next move. You've delved into the treasure trove of information and wisdom you have about yourself to see what sparkles and where the real value lies. You have created a full, detailed Career Profile which captures your best and favourite strengths and skills, what motivates and interests you and what meaningful and satisfying work is going to look like for you both practically and at a deeper level.

It's time to start exploring ways to put the pieces of the jigsaw together. To expand the ideas starting to bubble away. We're moving on from thinking about your now to your next. Or should I say *nexts* . . .

My Emerging Ideas

Areas of Real Interest
*e.g., sport, travel, fashion,
current affairs*

Themes That Keep Recurring
*e.g., creativity, leadership, risk-taking,
freedom, performance*

Skills I'm Keen to
Learn or Develop

Sectors I'd Love
to Investigate

Key Takeaways

Not all of us have a burning passion to follow in our work. Consider how important it feels to you to connect your professional identity to something that you have previously enjoyed as a hobby.

Your Interests can guide you in many ways – they can shape decisions about the kind of place you work, the skills you use or the clients you serve, just as much as directing you to a radical stand-alone passion project or entrepreneurial venture.

Take some time to think about your life as a whole – what has this chapter shown you about how you want to spend your free time as well as how you want to shape your career?

Action Checklist

- [ ] Unearth Your Interests
- [ ] My Emerging Ideas

Before You Move On

Fill in the Interests section on your Career Profile.

Your Career Profile is now complete and will be a valuable reference going forwards!

Step Three
Imagining and Designing

Let me liberate you from one of the daftest misconceptions in career design: that you're on a mission to find the perfect job, sitting there with your name on.

The thought that there is *one* magical option you need to find, a kind of holy grail of careers, is an unsettling and ultimately paralysing thought. Because – as I hear so often – 'What if I make the wrong decision?'

It sounds like a kind of Rumpelstiltskin-like torment to challenge you to find it. Come back in three days with the name of your perfect job or else.

Now, coming from someone who's written a book outlining the Five Steps to Finding Your Dream Job, that might sound a bit counter-intuitive. Isn't a dream job one that is perfect in every way? The job you want to take home and introduce to your mum? The job that you've pined for and fantasized about? That you've jealously looked at on the arm of a friend?

In fact, rather like choosing a life partner, finding the right job isn't about scouring the planet for absolute perfection, based on a fairytale idea that there is just one ideal person among the millions, waiting to be found by you. It's really about noticing *all* the options that pique your interest or set your heart racing a little faster and then exploring which ones feel like a potentially great match. The journey you're on is a bit like online dating, but fortunately without the pressure for a swimsuit pic.

What you've essentially just done through Step Two is fill in your 'profile' – you've uncovered a strong sense of who you are, what you're looking for and what you need to be fulfilled. You've put together a blueprint for a powerful pairing.

In this step, we're going to power up your imagination and generate intriguing *options*. You'll take full ownership of your existing and emerging ideas as well as learn creative, fun techniques to produce new ideas if needed.

We'll also look for potentially potent partnerships, great matches for the profile you've built, identify your favourites and where you want to start exploring.

But as we do so, I want you to embrace and enjoy the idea that there are many pathways you could happily and successfully take, rather than feeling stressed that you are heading towards a moment of trumpet-blasting decision that will irreversibly shape the rest of your life. A career change, big or small, is just the beginning of an ongoing journey, not the destination.

Relax, this is meant to be fun.

Chapter 7
Capturing and Generating Ideas

In this chapter, we're going to build a glorious, exciting list of career ideas. It's going to have *all* your ideas in it, from the obvious and relatively 'easy' to the wild daydreams that sit unspoken in your brain for fear of people laughing. It's likely to contain some fully formed ideas (high court judge, beauty-salon owner, yoga teacher, office manager), some vague ones ('something to do with heritage'), and possibly some weird niggly words that won't leave you alone but you don't yet know what to do with ('helping people').

What should this Ideas List look like? I want it to be exciting and inspiring. So now is the moment – if you're so inclined – to grab your coloured pens and a nice big piece of paper. Or your nicest notebook that you keep in your bag for moments of inspiration.

You might prefer an easily accessible Note on your phone, an orderly Excel spreadsheet or even a collage or a Pinterest board.

Do it in whatever way feels exciting, creative and full of possibility.

This list of ideas may well start messy, and that's fine. We'll refine and sort through it in Chapter 8.

What's important is to get all the possibilities out of your head and write them down. Why? Because it's time to take ownership of these ideas and let them see the light of day. Ideas that float about in your head remain nebulous and dreamy. Ideas that get captured on paper gain a degree of seriousness and become real options that require your attention and proper consideration.

TIP: Suspend 'Reality'

Your current view of what's 'realistic' or 'likely' kills possibility stone dead. Of course we're not in the business of devising a fantasy life that we'll never achieve, but if you listen too readily to the mind chatter that tells you things 'aren't possible', 'could never happen' or 'won't work', you're shutting a lot of doors and missing valuable ideas for a happy career.

Particularly in the early stages of this process, keep everything on the table. Engaging with the seemingly bonkers can lead to ideas that are far from hopeless. Each idea you have is like a bundle of possibility, a valuable source of information and inspiration for you, not a finite concept.

It's vital to remember that a big idea can be broken down into small steps which can make all the difference to a plan's viability. And building up to your very grandest career goals can potentially be done over years if you're happy to play the long game and build in periods of transition.

Let's get writing . . .

Are you already brimming with career ideas? If the work so far has you tripping over them in the hallway and the challenge is simply working out where you want to start investigating, feel free to spend just a short while here and then move on to Chapter 8. If your imagination needs a bit more of a workout, this chapter has all the kit you need to get your brain sweating. Take your time. Don't try and do all the exercises in one sitting. Spread them out and allow your idea muscles to build up in between.

You'll notice that some of the exercises focus initially on quantity not quality. Generating ideas is meant to be something of an unstoppable process. As the author John Steinbeck once memorably wrote, 'Ideas are like rabbits. You get a couple and learn how to handle them, and pretty soon you have a dozen.'

But a quick note. This is not about creating an avalanche of ideas that overwhelms you. Not every idea that you play with needs to make it into your final Ideas List. Trust your instinct. You'll know when you've hit on something that fizzes, and similarly you'll sense when you're forcing something.

The process I'm about to take you through is to first capture both the ideas that you already have and those emerging out of the self-reflection work you've done to create your Career Profile. Then I'll give you lots of ways to expand and develop them if you feel the need to generate more or flesh them out. If not, don't.

Let's bring your *existing ideas* out into the open. Write down any ideas that have been rattling around in your head for months or even years. They might feel fairly modest ideas, linked to your most recent role or your professional background, or they might seem dependent on you winning the lottery, undertaking serious retraining or relocating to another continent! Remember, no judgement. Put them on to the List.

If you've committed to doing the exercises in Step Two, there should also be lots of intriguing *emerging ideas* bubbling up just ready for you to capture next. Look back over the notes you've made at the end of Chapters 3 to 6. Your Emerging Ideas chart from the last chapter will be particularly valuable. Find the flashes of inspiration starting to emerge. These may currently feel like directions of travel rather than fully formed ideas. Don't worry if you're not sure what they mean right now or how your idea might become a specific job. We'll get to that in due course. Add anything that feels important to your Ideas List.

If your Ideas List looks a little sparse, vague or uninspiring, here are five creative approaches you can experiment with to produce a whole host of additional possibilities.

Ways to Expand Your Ideas and Generate More

Pick and Mix

A great way to really make the most of all the reflection you've done in Step Two is to play a game of Pick and Mix. Because you've realized that your ideal career is one which blends what you're interested in, what you're good at, what motivates you and how and where you'd love to work, so let's play around with that and see what comes up.

Grab a bunch of Post-it notes or cut up some sheets of card or paper into squares. Write out the key words or phrases from the four main sections of your Career Profile. The example opposite shows just four laid out in each group, but you'll have lots more.

Start by grabbing two Post-its or cards from different sections and putting them together on the table in front of you. You might start by taking one of your Interests and pairing it with your Ideal Environments. So in my example 'Classical Music' might pair with 'Respected Organization'. How many ideas can you generate with this combination? Let your imagination go wild. Write down everything that comes into your head. Hey presto, you're at the Albert Hall, BBC Radio 3 or the Royal Conservatoire of Scotland!

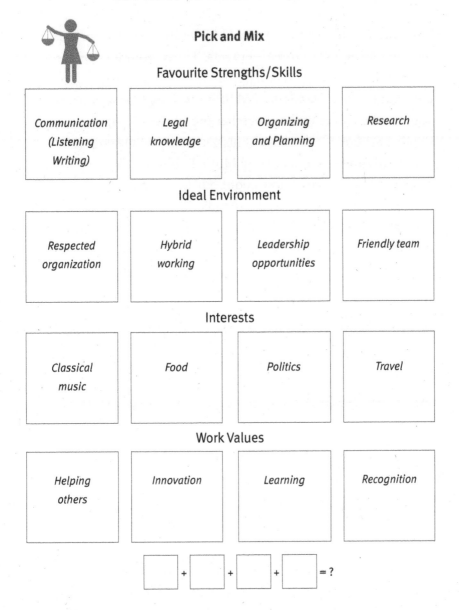

Pick and Mix

Favourite Strengths/Skills

Communication (Listening Writing)	Legal knowledge	Organizing and Planning	Research

Ideal Environment

Respected organization	Hybrid working	Leadership opportunities	Friendly team

Interests

Classical music	Food	Politics	Travel

Work Values

Helping others	Innovation	Learning	Recognition

[ ] + [ ] + [ ] + [ ] = ?

Play around with them. Swap the Environment for one of your Values, so you're now pairing 'Music' with 'Helping Others'. What's the result your brain can imagine? How about the Performing Rights Society or the Musicians' Union?

But what are you actually doing in these places? Time to add in an element of your Favourite Skills and see what comes up. Try pick and mixing with three elements. Throw your love of communication into the mix and perhaps you're doing PR or internal communications for Classic FM. If it's writing that stimulates you, maybe you're pulling together the student prospectus for the Brit School. If your legal skills get your day buzzing, how about in-house counsel at Sony Music Publishing? You are a great listener and musician – how about music therapy?

Again, have some fun and remember this is about expanding and generating ideas, however bonkers. Some combinations may not offer any new insights or generate new thoughts. Some might spark.

Sarah, who moved from working as a veterinary nurse to a soft tissue therapist in midlife, demonstrates brilliantly the pick-and-mix career.

You can read her full story on page 292, where you'll see that her new job is essentially a combination of what interests her (sports) with her skill set (medical knowledge, gym injury experience) and her ideal working environment (the flexibility and independence of her own business).

Mind Mapping

Whole books have been written on mind mapping techniques. You can check out the work of Tony Buzan – considered the father of mind mapping – if you want chapter and verse on the perfect way to do it. But at its simplest, a mind map is a visual tool designed to stimulate your brain and make connections in your thinking. Starting with one central concept, the aim is to use a single thought to spark lots of others.

Mind mapping can be a great tool if you have ideas that feel a little big or unwieldy and need further exploration. Look at your Ideas List for words that feel more like topics or themes than actual career paths. For example, Heritage, Tech, Helping People, Fashion.

Grab a big piece of paper and put that chunky theme in a bubble at the centre. Imagine your word is Food (see example below).

Next, let your mind throw up some key 'sub-sections' of that main idea (between three and seven) and use lines to branch out and create an evenly spaced ring of new words connected to your central idea. In the Food example, my mind offered me a number of very different food spin-offs from Education and Health to Recipes and Brands.

I then let the juices flow on each of those key areas in turn, spidering out more lines and ideas until I had a piece of paper bulging with thoughts and inspiration, breaking down each new

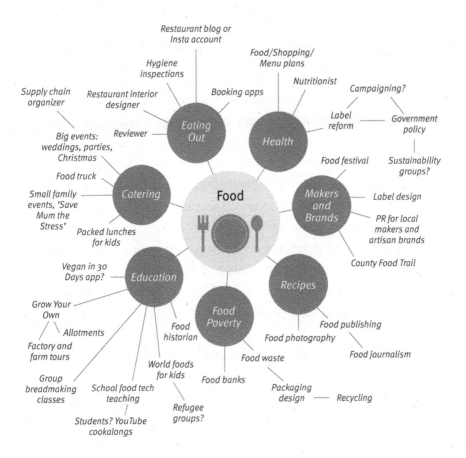

idea into new parts. I could have gone further. There's nothing to stop you creating even more outer rings (other than the size of your piece of paper!).

My quick mind map has shown a career based on an interest in food could include anything from allotment coordinator to nutritionist to food historian to recipe photographer. Let your imagination go wild.

Of course, not all of the spin-offs you create with a mind map need to go on to your Ideas List. In fact, worrying that every idea has to be a contender might hinder your imagination. Instead, use those guiding principles of 'Follow the Energy' and 'Suspend Reality' to decide which merit further exploration.

Brainstorming

Creative thinking can be hard to do on your own. Now is an excellent time to enlist the help of your best cheerleaders – be they friends or family – to throw in some new perspectives with a spot of brainstorming. This is an in-person group exercise, which can be done over coffee in the front room or sitting round the kitchen table with a drink or two! Ideally there would be between three and six of you. Two can feel too pressured and results in turn-taking rather than just diving in.

Approached with a few important ground rules, brainstorming is an effective way to expand and liberate your ideas from their normal straitjackets. Here are some long-established guidelines for a cracking brainstorm:

- Defer judgement: to allow creativity to flourish, you need to ditch any tendency to judge what comes up. At this stage, there are no bad ideas. Everyone gets to say what comes into their mind without comment, negative or positive. Give yourself permission to offer at least ten seemingly lousy ideas for every suggestion you're chuffed with.

- Be playful: really enjoy the wildest ideas. Sometimes there isn't as much of a gap between a crazy idea and a genius one as you might think.
- Build on other ideas: consider your job as a brainstormer not only to generate ideas yourself but to expand on other people's ideas. When someone suggests something, add the next layer, or make a sidestep. 'Yes, and' is a far more useful contribution than 'Yes, but . . .'
- Go for quantity: brainstorming is the mother of quantity over quality, and deliberately so. Crank your ideas out quickly and energetically.

Write it all down – nominate a note-taker to ensure no ideas are lost. If possible, write them on paper or sticky notes on the wall where everyone can see them.

For all its freedom, a successful brainstorm needs a specific prompt. The question 'What job could I do?' is too vague and too big. You will do better going a few times around with smaller questions.

Here are some ideas to help you get started:

Play It Straight

- How many ways could we find to help me use my skill/s of . . . ?
- How many ways could we think of to satisfy my interest in . . . ?
- Knowing the importance I place on _____, how many jobs can we devise where my values would be met brilliantly?

- What problems would I be perfect at solving?
- What organizations and places can we think of which are connected with _____ in any way?

Have Some Fun

- What is the craziest idea for a business I could run that plays to my strengths?
- What jobs could I do with my skills if money were no object?
- If I had to work at London Zoo/Parliament/the Ritz/ NASA, what jobs could I design for myself?
- If I had to work in another country, which country would it be and what would I be doing?

To avoid 'group think' and to ensure the session doesn't start hesitantly, allow a minute or two of quiet time for everyone to brainstorm a few ideas of their own in advance. Go around the room and let everyone share one of their ideas first before opening up the floor.

Try setting a timer for 10 minutes.

And don't stop early just because you hit silence and that feels embarrassing. It's when you have the sense that you are all out of ideas, that you are stuck, that you are forced to *really* think.

Once you've finished the brainstorm and you're sure there's nothing left unsaid, take a break. Come back to the notes on your own or as a group later to flesh out the best ideas and decide what should make it on to your Ideas List.

Hobby to Hero

This is an exercise designed to explore the many different ways you could interpret a basic idea that is swirling in your mind. Any idea you have could show up in your life with varying degrees of commitment. It could be just for fun or it could be building a multi-million-pound empire.

Take any less concrete ideas from your Ideas List and explore all the forms they could take, from simply being an activity you enjoy in your spare time or in a voluntary capacity to something you do full-time at the top of your game or where you have a Jeff Bezos-level budget. Playing around in this way not only generates specific ways to bring your idea to life, it also helps you consider the real attachment you have to it as a career prospect versus an activity for your spare time.

Hobby to Hero

Hobby	Volunteer	Beginner	Expert	Superhero
For fun, pleasure or interest	*Activity in your own time*	*Studying, starting out, working at a junior level*	*Established and working at a senior level*	*Thought leader, industry head, world domination!*

Here's an example for someone who has the idea of working in heritage in some way rattling around in their brain.

Hobby to Hero

Hobby	Volunteer	Beginner	Expert	Superhero
For fun, pleasure or interest	Activity in your own time	Studying, starting out, working at a junior level	Established and working at a senior level	Thought leader, industry head, world domination!
• Visit museums • Subscribe to BBC History Magazine • Join English Heritage • Attend annual heritage lectures • Listen to podcasts, e.g., You're Dead to Me • Blog on historic sites I visits	• National Trust working holiday • Help at stately home open day • Volunteer as tour guide at abbey • Write heritage column for local paper • Run history club at son's school	• Work in museum gift shop • Podcast producer for museum • UNESCO internship • MA Heritage Conservation • Web designer, local historic sites	• Museum curator • Archivist • Independent heritage consultant • Rare books librarian • HR for Landmark Trust • Events officer for art gallery • Lecturer in heritage studies	• Director General, UNESCO • Design billion-pound heritage app • CEO, Historic Scotland • Editor, BBC History Magazine

The added bonus of this exercise is that it can also help you think how you might chart a gradual course to your ultimate career ambition if it currently seems like a stretch. In Step Four we'll talk more about possible stepping stones to your career change – such as what you engage with in your free time, volunteering, studying or starting small.

Sector Surfing

The vast and ever-changing work landscape can be hard to get your head around if you've only ever worked in one area or have taken time out to raise a family and feel rather out of touch. It's a common frustration among the career curious that they 'just don't know what's out there'.

If you're struggling to think beyond your own experience but want to expand your horizons, why not try a spot of Sector Surfing? An easy way to do this is to look at the way jobs are grouped on vacancy websites. I've made it easy for you by pulling together my own Sectors List from a number of well-known job sites.

Administration	*E-commerce*	*Human Resources*
Animal Care	*Energy and Utilities*	*Insurance*
Artificial Intelligence	*Engineering*	*Information Technology and Telecomms*
Arts and Heritage	*Environment*	*Legal*
Banking and Currencies	*Farming and Food*	*Leisure*
Charities and Voluntary Sector	*Fashion and Beauty*	*Logistics*
Construction	*Financial Services and Accounting*	*Management*
Consultancy	*Further Education*	*Manufacturing*
Coaching and Counselling	*Government and Politics*	*Marketing and PR*
Communications	*Healthcare and Medicine*	*Media and Journalism*
Crime and Policing	*Higher Education*	*Motoring and Automotive*
Customer Service	*Hospitality and Events Management*	*Property*
Design and Creative	*Housing*	*Public Sector*
Digital Technology		*Purchasing*

Recruitment	Secretarial and PA	Social Work
Retail and FMCG (Fast Moving Consumer Goods)	Security and Cybersecurity	Sports
Sales	Skilled Trade	Technology
Schools	Social Care	Tourism and Culture
Science and Pharmaceuticals	Social Enterprise	Training
		Travel and Transport

First, simply surf your way over the sectors to see where you feel that tug of intrigue or excitement. You don't need to dive into any particular jobs themselves just yet. Which sectors leave you cold and which spark something? Then get your imagination into action.

An obvious first combination to play with is to take your current or most recent work and think what it would look like transplanted into a different sector. What difference could that make to your satisfaction levels? What opportunities could you foresee for someone with your skill set in one of these alternative fields?

If you are uncertain what kind of jobs exist in sectors you're not familiar with, then now's a good time to get curious. Visit some job sites and see what jobs appear under your favourite sectors. Here are some suggestions of places to start:

- https://www.monster.co.uk/
- https://uk.indeed.com/
- https://www.totaljobs.com/
- https://jobs.theguardian.com/
- https://www.adzuna.co.uk/
- https://www.reed.co.uk/
- https://www.escapethecity.org/

As ever, set aside all the 'buts' that are likely to start clamouring for your attention ('but all these jobs are full-time', 'but all these jobs are in London', 'but all these jobs need a science degree'). We are still looking at jobs as possibilities, collecting ideas that merit further investigation; we're not thinking about the so-called 'practicalities' or ruling things out based on negative assumptions your brain will be quick to offer you.

So get back to basics. Which jobs excite and interest you? Which feel like they are in sync with what you've been learning about yourself? Notice what elements of a job description particularly appeal to you.

LinkedIn is a valuable tool for helping you understand what jobs exist in different sectors. Enter a skill set and an industry (for example, 'marketing + travel' or 'teaching + hospitality') into the Job search. The results you are shown are a great way to learn about new companies, industry bodies and roles you weren't aware existed.

It can also be fascinating to use the People search function in the same way. Type your chosen skills and sector combination into the search box ('graphic design + healthcare') but this time select People. Hey presto, you can magically 'meet' a whole range of people who are working in this sphere in a myriad of different ways. It can be hugely enlightening to look at their profiles and see their career journeys – the places they've worked, the qualifications they've needed, the skills they highlight. And along the way you might even bump into someone who went to your college, lives in your local area or knows your old boss, which will serve you brilliantly when we get to Chapter 9.

Add any fresh ideas to your List. Don't worry if some of your ideas feel vague – we'll handle that in due course.

Widen Your World

Generating new ideas can be challenging if you aren't feeding your mind fresh information. Whilst I've shown that you can certainly make your brain work creatively with its existing store of data, you should also think about upping your consumption of original material. Or, as I like to call it, widening your world.

We tend to be creatures of habit, comfortable with our familiar world and our regular routines. We rarely break out of our default settings to expose ourselves to new environments, experiences, people or conversations.

So here are a few shifts you can make as you build your Ideas List to break away from tired thinking patterns that keep you uninspired.

Make a point of consuming different information. Grab a newspaper or magazine you've never read; watch TV programmes that aren't normally on your radar; try books away from your preferred genre; download an eclectic mix of podcasts; go to a talk or event that catches your eye; visit a museum, restaurant, festival, sports event or town you've never been to . . . Just by broadening your mind you allow new connections and ideas to form.

Ask other people about their work. I bet you have friends, siblings, even parents whose work you could barely describe. Get curious about what they do. Chat to them about their role, skills, responsibilities, organization, customers and so on. This isn't about wanting to do their job. Rather it's about widening your understanding of the world of work beyond your own well-trodden route and seeing what comes up.

Use the world around you as a giant set of questions. Whether you're on your local High Street, walking in the countryside, on holiday abroad, or sitting on the bus – open your eyes. Notice the jobs other people are doing, the organizations you come across, the people you meet, and ask yourself – what does that company actually do? Who works there? What problem are they solving? What would I enjoy about that job?

Key Takeaways

There is not only one perfect job with your name on – embrace the idea that there are numerous career pathways where you could find job satisfaction.

Ideas need to be captured and properly examined, not left floating around your brain.

Don't get caught up too early in what's 'possible' – the initial ideas process should feel expansive and exciting.

Use the principle of generating lots of ideas – even bad ones – to help you get closer to the meaningful and good ones.

Action Checklist

- ☐ Pick and Mix
- ☐ Mind Mapping
- ☐ Brainstorming
- ☐ Hobby to Hero
- ☐ Sector Surfing
- ☐ Widen Your World

Building your Ideas List is unlikely to be a one-day kind of process. Invest some quality time here. Revisit it, mull it over, play with it . . .

Chapter 8
Three Future Mes

In this chapter, you'll sort and prioritize your ideas. You'll check them against everything you've learnt about yourself and see which frontrunners are emerging.

It's unusual for career changers to have just one idea that they feel totally committed to at this stage. So why try to force yourself into an on-paper decision too early? The failed approach you've probably taken in the past – desperately trying to select one neatly mapped pathway before going all in – is exactly why you have picked up this book.

Instead, you're going to identify and really engage with the numerous versions of yourself vying for your attention.

What we'll create is three alternative 'Future Mes' that you'd like to try on for size. I encourage you to think in terms of *versions* of yourself rather than future *jobs* because it's quite likely that you won't immediately get to three exact job titles.

You might look at your Ideas List and say, 'What's emerging is that I want to be either a paramedic or a yoga teacher or a car mechanic . . .' If so, hurrah! You are streets ahead. In reality, I find this is unusual. I have rarely worked with a client whose Future Mes are all perfectly defined jobs. But if yours are, then you have something of a head start.

You're more likely to have a sense of three different *directions* you could see yourself moving in, three different worlds you could inhabit. One or two might be an exact job. Others might still be a concept. More on this in a moment.

Now, you may end up with fewer than three Future Mes if the fine-tuning you do here throws up a clear favourite or two. That's fine. Or you may have more! In theory, there's nothing to stop you investigating five, ten or every version of yourself you could imagine. In practice, it very much depends on how much time and energy you have to invest. And an extra caveat here – please bear in mind that time pressure can make a significant career change more challenging. If there is an urgency to your investigation (say looming redundancy or a toxic boss making work unbearable), you may need to think in terms of shifting jobs before you go for the full career change.

I'm about to walk you through some techniques to identify your favourite career ideas and sort them into three versions of yourself. But just before we dive in, a reminder that this is *your* process. If there are sorting exercises that don't add anything to your thinking or run counter to the way you feel you need to move forwards, leave them and organize your ideas in the way that feels meaningful to you. Career design is definitely more of an art than a science and the more you allow yourself to trust what comes up, the more powerful this exercise will be. You'll know your Future Mes when you see them.

Getting to Grips with Your Ideas List

Get your List in front of you and take a good look at it. How does it feel? Exciting? Cluttered? Nice and tidy? A bit confusing? Complicated or relatively straightforward? Vague or pretty detailed?

Here are a couple of examples from real career explorers:

Museum / Art Curator / Cataloguer

Educational Psychologist

Fundraising / Grants / Small charity / 'Purpose driven'

Media / Programme Researcher

Assistant Occupational Psychologist

Architectural Historian / Archivist / Historic Royal Palace

Alumni Network Coordinator

Obituary Writer / Biography Writer

Careers Advisor / Guidance / Interview Trainer/ ideas / CV help / training

Grief/ Bereavement/Supporting People/ using my own experience

Brain / Alzheimer's knowledge / Research

Start-up founder creative business (e.g., stationery)

Market Researcher – consumer trends / market insights

Veterans' charity / Imperial War Museum

Archivist / Family History / Genealogy – Who Do You Think You Are?

IDEAS LIST

I want to be: talking, listening, helping people, working with people

Talking therapy: Counsellor / Psychotherapist / Therapist / Wellbeing expert

Working for / creating content for a modern, exciting wellbeing brand, e.g., Headspace, Calm, Happy Not Perfect, Clementine, Heads Together

NHS roles: High Intensity Therapist, Psychological Wellbeing Practitioner, Clinical Psychologist, Health Psychologist

Psychology degree – positive psychology

Hypnotherapist / CBT / NLP / EFT Practitioner

Life Coach / Mindset Coach

A unique coaching angle like the Comparison Coach, Proof Coaching; Focusing on helping women like me at this stage of life; The Walking Therapist – combine my love of nature and therapy? E.g., Walk Leader Guide, Mental Health Mates

PND specialist, like Andrea Witt, The PND Coach

Nutritionist / Dietician

Occupational Therapist

Portfolio career – several fun interests, side hustles

Content / campaigns for environment agency, e.g., Woodland Trust, WWF, FoE

Women Returners Programme

Teacher (not school!) / Facilitator

MI5 / Civil Service / Intelligence

Radio / voiceovers

Media Researcher

Property expert

Travel Agent

When you are whipping it into shape to let your Future Mes emerge, I want you to consider the following:

- Which ideas generate real energy and enthusiasm?
- Which ideas sit best with all that you've discovered about yourself?
- Which ideas are actually all part of the same you and belong together?

Applying Your Three Brains

This is a great initial way of putting your ideas under the spotlight and sense-checking them against a number of important criteria.

Take each idea in turn and ask yourself the following questions:

HEART
How much do I like this idea?
How much does it excite and motivate me?

Where are ideas that you *love*? Which ones are your eyes drawn to? Which are jumping off the page? Which have a slight flatness or a lack of spark? In the flurry of creativity you've just gone through, it's possible that there are ideas that have made it on to your List that – on second thoughts – don't really get your juices flowing. Is it time to be brutal? Ditch anything that no longer feels right. Follow that energy!

GIVE EACH IDEA A HEART SCORE OUT OF TEN TO REFLECT YOUR LEVEL OF ENTHUSIASM

HEAD

How well does this idea fit with all that I've learnt
about myself and what's important to me?

You haven't just spent four chapters getting clear on what you want from your work and writing up a beautiful Career Profile only to shove it down the back of the sofa. This is super important. What do you *think* about the items on your list? Consider each of your ideas in the light of what you now know about the kind of skills you want to use, your areas of interest, the environment you want to work in and what makes you feel motivated and successful. Have you found a good match or are there likely to be important elements missing? You have created a mighty yardstick against which to measure your ideas. Use it.

GIVE EACH IDEA A HEAD SCORE OUT OF TEN TO REFLECT HOW COMPATIBLE IT FEELS TO YOUR CAREER PROFILE

GUT

What nagging feelings or niggling questions
come up for me around this idea?

Tap into your gut and you'll soon find your ideas come bundled up with a series of underlying sensations. See how you *feel* about each one. This score represents your confidence in an idea and your ability to make it a reality. A high score reflects a sense that this is well within your power. A low score indicates that something feels 'off' or potentially (but not necessarily insurmountably!) complicated. What you do with this information is up to you. Does a low score take it off the table? Or does it just raise your awareness about what might need to change and the timescale you need to factor in? If you find yourself wrestling with unhelpful assumptions and limiting beliefs, revisit Chapter 1 to reframe any concerns and see what impact that has.

GIVE EACH IDEA A GUT SCORE OUT OF TEN TO REFLECT HOW ACHIEVABLE IT FEELS

Your ideas all now have a score out of 30 that can help you prioritize, sort or cull!

Allowing Your Three Future Mes to Emerge

Depending on the size of your Ideas List and the effect of tapping into your three brains, you may now have your three Future Mes. If so, feel free to move on to 'Meeting Your Three Mes'.

However, if you're yet to see these fabulous potential versions of yourself waving back at you, perhaps it's time to cluster.

An Ideas List can – at first – appear like a series of slightly random thoughts. A kind of many-flavoured cocktail of jobs, alluring organizations and appealing concepts.

In reality, though, a deeper look reveals threads that run through them that can be woven together. Pulling some of your ideas together thematically can really help when an exact job is not yet clear but a direction of travel is.

As industries evolve, new sectors emerge and you consider unfamiliar worlds, it's understandable that you may struggle at this stage to name the exact job title you want to target within it. So if you're feeling curious but still a little unclear, don't panic or be put off.

Here are some common ways I've seen clients cluster their

ideas to create a possible Future Me or two, but don't be afraid to do it your way.

By Activity

You may have a group of ideas that come together thematically around what you see yourself doing, e.g., 'Helping Others' or 'Campaigning', but with a number of possible means of doing that.

So Helping Others Me is a neat way of capturing the emerging ideas you have around being a nurse, working for the Samaritans or training as a counsellor.

Campaigning Me may allow you to scoop up all your ideas about becoming an MP, being a press officer for Greenpeace, writing for the *Big Issue* or working in a women's refuge.

Different jobs. Same you. Can you see a way to group a number of different potential roles under one particular version of yourself that you want to explore?

By Sector

You may have several ideas that sit under the umbrella of a particular sector or industry, for example 'Education' or 'Fashion' or 'Public Health' or 'Charity'.

Take the 'Fashion' example: you're not yet clear whether you want to take your existing marketing job into the fashion industry or find a way to use your growing photography skills or launch your own fitness clothing line, but you know that there is a Fashion Me that certainly merits investigation.

Or an Education Me cluster may encompass a secondary school teacher, private maths tutor or working as an education officer at a museum.

By Way of Working

You might find your ideas naturally cluster around a method of working. So there might be a Freelance Me, a Corporate Me or perhaps an Entrepreneurial Me that neatly pulls together several possible ideas that you can't yet choose between. Do you have ideas that want to sit under one of these Future Mes?

By the Scale of Change

Some people like to think of their career possibilities on a kind of spectrum, grouping them in terms of how radical a move they represent. I'm positive you have ideas you'd consider pretty obvious but that you've never quite got round to, some that feel a bit different but still related to your background, and others that are quite radical.

You might like to try ordering your ideas in this way, though it's crucial to try to treat each spot on the spectrum equally and not get lured into using words like 'safe' or 'easy' options as opposed to 'unrealistic' or 'daydream scenario'. That can quickly turn into an off-putting shorthand that some options are boring and some are impossible.

To avoid that, take a look at the scale of change overleaf and see where your ideas fit along it.

If you want to experiment with sorting your ideas like this, it can be useful to try answering the following questions too:

- Where do I naturally sit on this scale?
- Am I more drawn to ideas that require minor alterations or a dramatic change?
- How would I need to think or behave differently if I wanted to change my 'default' settings?

If this way of organizing your ideas appeals to you, think how you might name your three Mes – perhaps 'Improved Caroline' – 'Different Caroline' – 'Go It Alone Wild Caroline'.

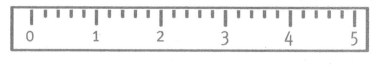

Refine ⟶ Refocus ⟶ Reinvent

Ideas here involve a simple TWEAK or two

Ideas here could be described as a PIVOT

This is for ideas involving a RADICAL MOVE

Everyone has at least one of these ideas. Essentially it means sticking with what you're currently doing but with minor tweaks to make it as fulfilling as possible based on all that you've learnt about yourself so far.

Empowered by that new knowledge, you are thinking about some relatively straightforward changes to REFINE what you are doing.

Ideas here might include seeking additional or different responsibilities, going for a promotion, asking for some in-house training or professional development opportunities to ramp up your favourite skills, going part-time/ full-time or becoming self-employed/ staff.

Collect ideas here that take your established profession and switch an element of it in a significant way.

A career PIVOT often means taking your existing job to a totally different sector or organization which is unfamiliar but appealing.

You might be an accountant for a big corporate firm but would like to be an accountant for a start-up or in the charity sector.

Or, conversely, a pivot can mean staying in your industry but taking on a totally new type of role.

So you're a PA for a fashion brand but would love to become a buyer there instead. It's a shift, but within a world that is at least partly known.

This is where you put the big shifts.

A REINVENTION is a whole new career, either partly or wholly unconnected to what you have done to date (at least on the surface).

Setting up your own new business from scratch is another one.

An idea about a large chunk of retraining or a big course of study might well sit here.

All in all, it's a rebranding of your career and who you are.

Meeting Your Three Mes

Who are these three people who stand before you? Let's get to know them.

Whatever the current shape of your Three Mes, I want you to give them some sparkling personality before we move on. Creating a colourful picture around each one will help you get to know who you are dealing with and understand the life they are potentially offering you.

Painting a picture of the three lives you could live might seem an unusual exercise but try it and you are likely to find it both dynamic and enlightening. Like your ideal work vision, this exercise can channel your energy and focus on to what you want and give you something far more 'real' to work towards.

So, I want you to truly inhabit each of these versions of yourself in turn. Take yourself to a point in the future where you have *become* that person and picture that new life as if you are really living it. So not 'I imagine myself doing x' but 'I *am doing* x'.

Go for full technicolour. Imagine this new Me has worked out brilliantly and describe what you see. If your Me is based on a theme rather than a specific job, that's fine. You can include some variations, e.g., I'm working in the fashion industry, as x, y or z.

Set a timer for 5 minutes and scribble down as much detail as you can about the first Me. If you find it hard to get started or need some prompting, try responding to some of these sentence openers.

- I am working . . .
- My day is filled with . . .
- The people around me are . . .
- This means I can . . .

- I love it because . . .
- It brings me . . .
- It plays to my skills of . . .
- It meets my values of . . . by . . .
- The best thing about this work is . . .
- It gives me . . .
- Those around me tell me . . .
- I'm able to say to myself that . . .
- I'm feeling . . .
- I've managed to get to this point by . . .
- I have ambitions to . . .
- I am often asked to . . .
- My favourite part of the day is when . . .
- The joy of this role is . . .

TIP: Recognizing How You Do Your Best Thinking

If writing isn't your thing, then try using your phone to film or voice-record yourself talking through this vision. Don't overthink or try to make it perfect. Just allow the words to flow. It might help to shut your eyes.

Or ask one of your cheerleaders to listen to you talking this through. They can start by simply asking, 'Take me into a future where you are living that first possible life working as a . . . or in the field of . . .' and, if you start to slow down, they can use the prompts to form questions to stimulate your thinking. They should take notes of everything you say for you to use afterwards.

Repeat the exercise for each of your Three Mes and once you have your stream of pictures, your raw material, spend some time working it into a written vision that feels exciting.

Give each Me a name or a title (Supporting Women Me . . . Creative Me . . . Prema the Garden Designer . . . Prema the PR Expert) to powerfully capture that particular vision.

So now you have up to three visions. What did you notice as you described each one?

For Caroline – a solo parent considering her options after a career break – the process of taking herself into the future added some extra insight and clarity about where she should be directing her energy.

Describing 'Improved Caroline' – recreating her old marketing job with just a few changes – actually felt a little dull and wasn't really doing it for her.

'Go It Alone Wild Caroline' – setting up her own business as an events manager – felt exciting but something for her longer-term future. Not to be discounted, but too big a leap for her right now.

Whereas 'Different Caroline' – taking her marketing skills out of the finance sector and into either the arts or charity sphere – brought her the energy she was looking for.

So Caroline had her focus. She decided to move forwards with just one Future Me and to concentrate her next steps on really investigating a move into the arts.

What you do is up to you. You can take three Future Mes forwards to work on concurrently, address them in turn or just concentrate on the one you have realized is really desperate to meet you.

However you choose to proceed, there's really only one way to find out what's going to work . . . remember what I said back at the start of Step Two about the second biggest mistake in career redesign? You're about to tackle it as you move on to Step Four.

Key Takeaways

Some of your Ideas may be fully formed jobs, some may be more conceptual or thematic – look for ways to group your ideas if that feels more manageable.

Use your Career Profile to see which ideas feel the most authentic and meaningful in the light of what you've established about yourself.

Ideas can call to you in different ways – it's good to notice which ideas feel most exciting, which feel most practical and which feel most in keeping with all you know about what you want.

Identifying and exploring up to Three Future Versions of yourself is a much less stressful and a far more practical approach to career change than trying to decide on one perfect job on paper or in your head.

Action Checklist

☐ Applying Your Three Brains

☐ Sorting and Grouping Ideas

☐ Meeting Your Three Mes

Step Four
Taking Action

When I met Helen she was stuck. Now in her early forties, she had spent more than a year mulling over the different lives she might live. On the one hand, she was drawn to child art therapy. On the other, she had the opportunity to develop a residential arm for her husband's fine art studio, which was currently focused on commercial businesses.

Helen had two Future Mes. On paper, both stacked up pretty well against her interests and skills. Both offered her the chance to work flexibly and fulfil her need to feel valued and have her 'own thing' outside of home. Both also raised questions she was unsure about.

So she was stuck in the dreaded analysis paralysis. Making the classic mistake of believing you can *think* your way into a career redesign. Seeing two very different pathways stretch out in front of her, and allowing them to simply bang about in her brain, a creaking seesaw of worries and excitements, pros and cons.

Now I know I've just urged you to spend a tasty chunk of time getting curious about yourself and your situation. I believe thinking and reflecting as an initial step is vitally important.

But you stop there at your peril. Because the most powerful piece of your career redesign is to build on that brain work with some leg work. By getting into action.

What did I advise Helen to do? Find small but practical ways to try out both of her Future Mes. My strong view was that she should speak to as many people as she could and try to see these careers in action – I put her in touch with a local friend of mine who was working in children's mental health and encouraged her to invite this friend for a coffee. She soon realized she knew three or four people herself – including her husband's brother – who had either direct links to young people's therapy or knew people who worked in the field. 'Once I started looking, opportunities to investigate seemed to crop up everywhere and I was able to ask lots of questions about the training and the work and what people did and didn't like about it. I even discovered an art therapy bus.' Meanwhile, Helen was also spending odd mornings here and there working for her husband's business, trying that on for size.

Trying to make a career decision without giving something a go is like trying to work out if you'll like skiing without ever setting foot on the slopes. Yes, you can collect some valuable and relevant information – you liked sledging as a kid, the French Alps look beautiful and you're a pretty decent skater . . . but until you actually strap on a pair of skis, you really can't know for sure.

Or to return to an online dating analogy, some things are not what they seem and it takes a painful evening of stilted conversation and warm white wine to realize it. What's flashy and alluring on the surface doesn't always create an authentic connection. What seems perfect on paper turns out in person to be nothing like you imagined.

There are uncertainties, gaps in your knowledge and a colourful smattering of assumptions that could do with being tested. The key thing with any partnership, whether in love or in career redesign, is not to dive in headfirst and make a massive commitment without first giving it a whirl.

I'm going to show you how to undertake low-risk, low-investment ways to investigate if your vision matches the reality. After all, it would be as unwise to sign up for a three-year degree in fashion design simply because you like *The Great British Sewing Bee* as it would be to get married based on one gorgeous photo. In both cases, you're likely to find out six weeks in that it was a horrible mistake.

Helen is now taking a one-year foundation course in art therapy and thoroughly enjoying it. When we catch up, I ask her to reflect on how people could approach their early explorations. It takes her all of ten seconds. 'Ask the people you talk to if you could observe their art therapy sessions in action. See if you can go and visit a counselling centre.'

So this is where we get up close and personal with your Future Mes. We set out to properly meet them – take them on a date, do stuff with them, ask all of our burning questions and really get to know them.

Then, once you have the best information you can get and you're confident you're nearing the 'one', we'll set the goals to bring you together for good.

What do you most need for Step Four? I respectfully refer you back to my Three Cs: Commitment, Courage and Curiosity. This is where they will really come into their own.

- Commit regular time and energy to the investigations you are about to embark on.
- Be courageous about doing things that challenge you.
- And, above all, be as curious, open-minded and enthusiastic as you possibly can.

There's a chance you might feel this is starting to get 'serious'. Actually, this is about to get fun. The greatest thing you can do is to approach this lightly and, dare I say, playfully. Throw off any sense of pressure to decide and embrace the adventure of finding out.

You're moving into explorer mode.

Because let me tell you something quite revelatory and a little bit counter-intuitive right now. Even when you've selected these career paths you want to investigate, the chances are that the destinations you're currently imagining are not *exactly* where you'll actually end up. I don't mean that you'll start off planning to be a prison officer and become a beautician (though it happens), but the journey itself will definitely strongly shape the journey's end.

What you find out, the experiences you open yourself to and the people you meet on your upcoming travels will intrigue you, surprise you, excite you and challenge you. But the most potent thing they will do is to *empower* you to make a far better decision about where you want to go.

Chapter 9
Trying on Your Future Mes

There are six words every one of my clients will say at some point that trigger a high-pitched warning sound in my brain.

'I need to do some research.' BEEP-BEEP-BEEP-BEEP. Can you hear that?

It's generally the first answer you'll reach for when I ask how you can find out more about your fabulous new Me career idea.

And invariably, by research, you mean Google.

Ah, the simplicity of sitting at your desk with a nice cup of coffee and typing your question into a search engine. How comfortable, how safe, how . . . dull and ineffective.

'How do I become a dog trainer?'

'What qualifications do you need to work in marketing?'

'What do web developers do?'

'How much can a virtual assistant earn?'

It's quite extraordinary how many hours we can spend on internet searches only to end up not much clearer than we were before, and possibly more muddled. I'll bet you even find yourself returning to the same ten websites on a regular basis with some peculiar expectation that you'll unearth something different. Are you really surprised you're not making any progress?

I have news. For anything more than some initial facts (and sometimes not even that) Google just won't cut it for your career investigation. It's time for some new approaches.

I'm going to give you the four kinds of meaningful research experiments you should do instead and I should warn you now that – sorry – there no armchairs involved. Focusing predominantly on active rather than passive means of research is what will finally move you forwards.

But before we start looking for the answers you need, take some time to write down all the questions you have.

Each of your Future Mes comes with a side helping of unknowns, uncertainty and hidden assumptions. Now is also the moment to dig out any of those practical 'buts' from Chapter 1.

Some will be quite broad. For example, 'Would I enjoy this work?', 'Does it actually play to my strengths?' and 'What does this job actually involve day-to-day?'

Others will be much more specific. Such as 'Does everyone in this industry have an engineering background?', 'Could I make this work as a part-time job?' or 'Is a pay cut inevitable?'

Here are some examples:

Marketing Me	Journalist Me	Entrepreneur Me
How would I move from sports to fashion?	*Would a formal qualification be helpful?*	*Would I like working on my own?*
Are there returnship programmes?	*Would I prefer writing or podcasting?*	*How do you find investors?*
Is agency or in-house more interesting?	*Are newspapers already dead?*	*How long will it be before I start earning?*
Where are the growth opportunities?	*How do freelancers get commissioned?*	*Does my idea have legs?*

As you go through your process of investigation, you can keep adding to your list. New pieces of information will throw up additional questions, open up a related idea you hadn't previously considered or highlight a gap in your knowledge you'd like to rectify.

Now naturally some of the answers you get will delight and motivate you. That's great. Keep following up and colouring in the vision. Others might at first disappoint or demoralize you and this risks derailing your exploration. There's an important thing to remember. All new information is valuable and actionable.

Should you discover that something isn't as great/easy/interesting as you thought, don't fall into the trap of thinking you've failed. Whilst it can feel a bit gutting that you don't actually love dog grooming with the passion you envisaged, you have still made progress. You've struck something off the list, allowing you to keep moving forwards rather than vaguely chasing a dream around in your head.

More commonly, though, the outcome is more nuanced than a big fat yes or no. Say your research makes you realize you still love dogs but you just don't love grooming them when they are wet and smelly. That's not a closed door, simply time for a new question, such as, 'What other examples can I find of people working with dogs?' or 'Could I use my business skills to run a dog grooming business but hire staff to do the actual grooming?' Similarly, finding out that becoming a psychotherapist takes six years of expensive study doesn't have to signify the end of your enquiry. The question may simply need to shift. 'What other ways of working in talking therapies exist?' or 'How could I keep working to fund a course of study at the same time?' Keep in mind those 'Go Below' techniques from Chapter 2. What does that tell me? How significant is this?

Remember, this is a journey of discovery. Not everything will fall brilliantly into place, not everyone will say yes, but the more you step into new places and situations, the more you allow the career gods a little room to manoeuvre.

Researching and Testing

On to the four methods of active research to test your Future Mes. You are starting on an exciting experimental project! You should set aside several weeks as a minimum, but it could well take several months or more. I'd go so far as to state that the commitment and dedication you invest at this point is directly linked to how confident and clear you feel moving forwards later down the line. So get stuck in.

You'll quickly see how all of these methods of research overlap and how they have the power to:

- Help you build real knowledge of and familiarity with the career you're considering.
- Grow your confidence about what is right for you.
- Forge interesting connections with people who have the potential to help you.
- Give you first-hand experience of the work in mind.
- Get more comfortable talking about yourself and your plans.
- Open up further pathways and opportunities.

We're going to start with the biggie, because in many ways it underpins everything else.

1. Curious Conversations

Not long ago, a client of mine, Kate, sent me an email that made me beam. A 46-year-old journalist and copywriter, Kate, was considering a career as a counsellor and I'd sent her and her fellow group of coachees away with clear instructions to stop googling and start talking.

> 'I thought I'd share that I had a fantastic week this week. What a contrast to last week, which was so difficult and dispiriting. As you say, the magic is in the people. I have had a couple of really useful conversations and breakthroughs!'

If I was forced to share just one thing about career redesign, it would be that.

The magic is in the people.

Other people have information and insight that cannot be found in any browser. They have real-life experience. And the joy of other people is that they are gloriously interactive.

I know this space can feel intimidating. One client, Naya, had a definite block around this. 'I don't feel ready yet,' she told me. 'I'll go and have some conversations when I have a better idea about what's involved in the job.' 'And how are you going to find that out,' I grinned, 'if you don't *ask* anyone?'

Your biggest research tool is talking – to people who do what you want to do, people who are familiar with the place or industry you'd love to work in, people who have the skills you want to have, people who have walked the pathway you'd like to walk.

That's what you're aiming for. Now I know exactly what happens next. You're going to hit me with one of two excuses. Quite probably both:

- 'I hate networking and I'm rubbish at it.'
- 'I don't know anyone who does what I want to do!'

Nope, not accepting either of those. Here's why:

'I hate networking and I'm rubbish at it.'

This is not networking. Or at least, it could be, but not if your response to the concept of networking is a negative one. I've deliberately resisted that word, knowing that it may fill you with fear or horror. Very often, the idea of networking is bound up with images of stiff professional events and swapping business cards, alpha male lunches and golf clubs, or the pressure to sell yourself, wow someone or make fawning requests for favours. And you think you're rubbish at it because you wrongly assume you need something to trade or a kickass pitch to roll out.

Actually, there are far better definitions of authentic and modern networking, such as the very simple concept of building relationships.

Regardless, ditch the notion of networking and embrace the idea of conversations. That's all I want you to have. Curious Conversations. We'll come to what they look like in a minute, but let's tackle that other excuse first.

'I don't know anyone who does what I want to do!'

When I ask people who they know who works in a particular field (unless it's something similar to their own background) they are usually quick to assume they don't know anyone. But that's because your brain is lazy.

Firstly, it's only scanning the handful of people you see regularly, your inner circle of family and long-standing mates. And secondly, it's got them neatly filed under two very narrow labels – their relationship to *you* and what they are doing *now*. See if you recognize this kind of mental filing system:

- JEN – sister – looking after small baby, career break from teaching
- JOEL – brother-in-law – tech bod of some kind, can't remember what sector, maybe energy?
- SAIRA – uni mate – lawyer in something I don't understand to do with patents or copyright
- RICHARD – colleague – HR consultant

And on it goes. Neat, but unimaginative.

So I need you to expand your Circle of Connections to allow your brain to scan a much bigger list for potential conversationalists. Take a look at the model below to see just how enormous your world can be.

My Circle of Connections

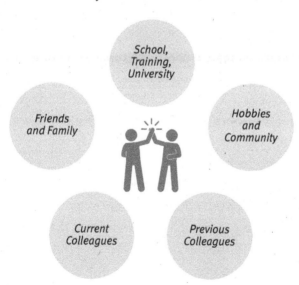

Draw your own five circles and start filling them with the names of all your connections. Don't exclusively think about your Future Mes and whether you believe there is any link. Just open your mind to all the people you are connected to, be that closely or loosely.

Family should include not just your parents (they are not as past it as you think) and your siblings but your fabulous Aunt Louise and cool Cousin Niall too. Friends will of course include your very dearest, but what about all the people you know on Facebook, like your one-time housemates from your twenties or people you met travelling? School, Training or University could include classmates, people you were in clubs or on committees with as well as friends or even teachers and lecturers. Think about whether there is an alumni association that holds a list of who's now doing what. And don't overlook training courses you went on, either academically or professionally. Hobbies and Community can be anything from your hockey team and yoga friends to your street WhatsApp group, and people you've met through antenatal class, your son's judo club and your school-gate network. Think broadly.

Just by getting creative about the range of people you know, you've probably spotted someone you'd overlooked who could hold some insight into a Future Me. You've remembered your neighbour three doors down is a nurse or your vicar used to be an investment banker. Fantastic. You're ready to ask for a Curious Conversation.

If no one has immediately jumped out at you, fear not.

When you have your Circle of Connections, consider this – every person sitting in one of *your* circles is at the centre of five circles of their very own. So even if you only put a measly two people in each of the five sections, that already has the potential to link you to a hundred people!

And you have no idea of the connections other people can make for you. You don't know what you don't know. So your techy brother-in-law Joel may be just one thing to you, doing whatchamacallit in the energy sector. But how do you know that his old housemate isn't a fashion buyer or working in charity PR or running their own graphic design business?

Remember Kate and the magic of people? This is how her email went on:

> 'There have been some rather strange and wonderful coincidences. My husband happened to look over my shoulder as I was reading the website for the counselling course I've applied to and saw a photo of one of the previous students and said, "I know her!" Turns out that one of his first managers has also retrained as a counsellor and she is now top of my list to contact this week. A sign?'

Definitely. So go and find those connections.

Here are some guide templates you might find helpful.

You can use an informal email like this (or WhatsApp message or personal Facebook or Instagram post etc.) to spread your Curious Conversation request far and wide in the form of a challenge. You might take a 'send to all' approach or start by approaching one group of connections. Kate focused on her old antenatal-class group, where she felt most comfortable and relaxed, to make the request.

> *Dear ,*
>
> *I'm contacting you with a challenge! As you may know, I'm taking some time to consider the next chapter in my working life and I'm exploring options for a career return/redesign/change.*
>
> *One of the avenues I'm exploring is . . .*

Or

I'm currently investigating (1/2/3) possible sectors/jobs/types of work. [List them]

So I'm asking my brilliant network WHO DO YOU KNOW (or who do you know who is sure to know someone) who works in this field and would be happy to talk to me?

What I'm after is a 30-minute chat over coffee/Zoom in the next month to tell me about their own route in and share their overview of their job and the industry.

I've set myself a challenge to speak to ten people and I'd love you to help me reach that number.

It would be brilliant if you could suggest one person you know and put us in touch.

If you need a slightly more formal approach, for former colleagues or people you aren't regularly in touch with, you could modify it to ensure you invest some time reconnecting and replace the light-hearted challenge element with a sense of a career research 'project' that you are embarking on.

Dear ,

Start with a warm, personalized approach which re-establishes your connection and demonstrates an interest – make sure it's genuine!

I recently read your LinkedIn post about . . .

I was talking to _____ last week and was reminded of the project we all did on _____.

I've been following your brilliant new business on Instagram . . .

Give some very *brief* context if it feels appropriate to remind them about yourself:

*After x years with A Company/on a career break/redundancy
. . . I'm considering taking my love of x or experience/skills in x
and transitioning into y . . . You'll no doubt remember my obsession
with all things digital/my passion for PowerPoint/my desire to
have our away day in Vienna!*

One of the avenues I'm exploring is . . .

Or

*I'm currently investigating (1/2/3) possible sectors/jobs/types
of work. [List them]*

*So I'm reaching out to my wider network to ask who they know
who works in this field who would be happy to talk to me?*

*I'm setting out to talk to a range of people in a series of
30-minute Zoom chats/coffees over the next month. The aim is a
relaxed conversation about that person's own career journey and
their insights into their job and the shape of the wider industry.*

No challenge scenario needed here, just a professional,
methodical approach.

*It would be brilliant if you could suggest one person you know
who would fit the bill and I'd be delighted if you were able to make
an email introduction.*

All wisdom gratefully received!

TIPS: Approaching a Curious Conversation with Conviction
However you choose to express your request, here are some
important pointers.

Position yourself as an explorer or investigator. You are not asking for a job or selling yourself. You are in curious mode. Taking this role avoids the fear or embarrassment that often arises when you think you need to know stuff in order to talk to people about your Future Me. That's the whole point. You are there to learn and by using phrases like 'I'm investigating/exploring' you take away the pressure to have all your ducks in a row.

Avoid sounding apologetic or embarrassed. Too many emails begin with phrases like 'I hope you don't mind me contacting you . . .' or 'Sorry if this is a big ask . . .' and end with the sentiment 'I totally understand if it's too much bother'. This is a time for communicating with clarity, enthusiasm and conviction – even if you don't yet fully feel it!

Make a clear ask: who do they know who would meet you for a conversation and can they put you in touch. If you write 'I'm wondering if you might possibly know someone who perhaps has a sense of . . .', you've lost your audience. Their brain will do what yours did and tell them they don't know anyone. Write assuming that they do know someone and their brain will work harder to find that person. Then make them sure of what you'd like: a 30-minute conversation in the next month. All this focuses the mind.

Don't over-elaborate or overshare: Keep it short, factual and upbeat. At this stage there's no need for a massive job history and certainly no call for your career break woes or redundancy saga. Avoid the temptation to share complexities or worries around your situation like 'I suspect it's going to prove difficult to move given my background so I want to check . . .' Stop it!

Practise on your 'warmest' connections. As you grow in confidence and knowledge, you'll be able to take those

Curious Conversations into less familiar territory, but for now, you want to start in a comfortable space to perfect your questioning skills. If you're unsure, start with personal connections before you move to more professional ones. The first person to approach for Journalism Me is not the editor of Red magazine, even if she's your aunt's best friend. It's your brother's girlfriend who runs a successful blog. Work your way up and save the biggies until you feel you're really motoring.

Once you've got some candidates for a Curious Conversation, you're ready to get into action. Unsure what this conversation should look like? From your point of view, pretty quiet! You should actually do very little talking. It's all about great questions and strong listening, with the aim of finding out about the reality of a particular job and sector. Here's a loose structure to experiment with.

Outline the connection

If needed, remind them how their work or background connects with what you are interested in and how you came to be in touch ('Thanks so much for answering my friend Joanna's call for healthcare experts!' or 'Your colleague Simon and I used to work together at X Company and I'm really pleased that you are happy to talk to me about the world of HR'.)

Set the tone and the expectation

Remind them that you are talking to a number of people about a line of work that you're considering and want to hear their experience and insights. You won't keep them for more than 30 minutes.

Use simple, open questions

Open questions like these invite informative expansive answers:

- How did you get into the work you do?
- What other routes in do you see?
- What does your typical day / week involve?
- What do you find most enjoyable about the work?
- What is challenging or difficult about the role?
- What's it like to work here?
- What do you wish you'd known when you started out?
- What kind of person do you think does well in this line of work?
- How do you see this kind of work evolving?
- What are the big conversations going on in the industry right now?

Create onward momentum

Wrap up by asking for a suggestion for the next step on your journey. 'That's been so helpful, thank you. I'm aiming to talk to a range of people about this – who else do you think would be a great person to chat to? or 'Where else should I definitely be investigating?' or 'Which do you think are the key organizations to get familiar with?'

THINGS TO AVOID

Talking too much about yourself

Don't waste this precious information-gathering opportunity by giving your life story. It's natural that at some point you may be asked about yourself and what you're hoping to do. You may even worry about this, as you're still not totally sure!

So prepare a simple three-sentence overview, based on your background, a key skill or interest and your potential future.

Whilst you're not there to sell yourself, mentioning something you're good at can help you sound positive and confident:

- I spent ten years in HR before a planned career break and a massive house renovation. Now I'm looking at ways to combine my extensive people management skills and my passion for property development. I'm investigating the residential property sector to see where I might find an interesting fit.
- I've worked as both a PA and VA, mostly within education. My admin and communication skills are really strong and I'm great under pressure! But actually, I do a lot of volunteering for my local hospice and it's made me consider a move into nursing of some kind.

Don't ever couch your journey in negative terms – 'I can't stand my boss so I really need to move on' or 'I've realized I'm not cut out for high-pressure environments, so I'm wondering about yoga teaching'.

Asking for obvious information

This is your chance to get this person's unique and personal take. Don't ask factual questions about the organization or person that a simple Google or LinkedIn search would give you. Do a bit of homework beforehand to cover the basics. Some prior knowledge will make you look more professional too.

Overrunning

Respect their time. Be ready to bring the conversation to an end as soon as your 30 minutes is up. If they offer to keep going, great, otherwise stick to what you promised. They are unlikely to connect you to other people if what was billed as a 30-minute coffee turned into an hour-long grilling.

CHALLENGE

Ten Thank You Cards

Ready for those Curious Conversations? Hold yourself to it. Go out and buy ten thank you cards. This not only creates a clearly defined goal to speak to ten people but is also a genuinely thoughtful touch and a good way to build a relationship. As we'll see in Chapter 10, the conversations you have now can sometimes sow seeds that later blossom in unexpected ways.

The best notes are more than a quick line of thanks. Aim to highlight what was useful, what you are going to do with the information you gained and mention keeping in touch.

> Dear Geoff,
>
> Thanks so much for meeting me on Monday to talk about your garden design business. It was inspiring to see your studio set-up and the plans for that stylish water garden – good luck with the tricky fountain system!
>
> Your advice about the Royal Horticultural Society was invaluable and I've just signed up for their Taster Day.
>
> I've also dropped a note to Sarah to arrange to visit the community project you mentioned to see if there are some volunteering opportunities.
>
> I will let you know how I get on.
>
> Best wishes,
>
> Rebecca

Connecting with other people is something that Katherine did a lot of when she considered shifting from marketing into website design as she hit her fifties. She even made connections online.

'Don't be afraid to ask people for help even if they are complete strangers. My experience is that if it is a genuine ask and you're nice about it and you're respectful of people's time, they will often say yes. And if they say no, don't worry – someone else will say yes. I've reached out to people in the US – Squarespace and web designers whose work I've seen and admired – and said, "I'm interested in your journey, I'm trying to do the same thing, what do you think?" and they've been really nice and friendly. There are lots of web design Facebook groups where you can seek advice or ask for guidance.'

I've spent a long time equipping you for Curious Conversations. That's because I'm evangelical about their power in testing your Future Me.

But there are still three other methods for you to get cracking on.

2. Lean Learning

Lean Learning is a research approach all about finding relatively short and low-cost opportunities to investigate a new skill, specialism or course of study that could be important to a Future Me.

If you are considering training as a graphic designer, your first move isn't to decide whether to do a twelve-month diploma or a three-year BA. Hold your horses. Do you even know the five basic principles of design?

Lean Learning opportunities can be found all over the place.

Short courses needn't cost a lot of money and may only require an evening a week for a term, a weekend for an initial 'Introduction to . . .' or an even shorter Taster Day.

A good place to start is the adult education programme offered by your local authority or courses offered by your local further education college. Both tend to have a hefty range of subjects from childcare, accounting and coding to languages, creative writing, catering and counselling. Check out the Continuing Education department at your local university, which will be packed with short courses. In fact, these days you don't even have to limit yourself to what's local, given the opportunities for virtual learning.

The last few years have seen an explosion of so-called MOOCs, which stands for Massive Open Online Course. MOOCs are generally free or low cost and are run by some of the world's top institutions – think Harvard, Berkeley, Cambridge University, the Sorbonne . . . They're a low-risk way to explore your inner designer, philosopher, teacher, coder, accountant, fashion manager, nutritionist . . . They don't always lead to formal qualifications, but they're a great place to dive in and are generally self-paced, meaning you can fit in your learning in a way that suits you and do as much or as little as you want.

You'll find examples of MOOCs here:

- https://www.edx.org/
- https://www.futurelearn.com/
- https://www.coursera.org/
- https://theskillstoolkit.campaign.gov.uk
- https://www.udemy.com/
- https://www.open.edu/openlearn/

LinkedIn Learning is another place worth a look, boasting 'over 16,000 online courses taught by real-world professionals'. To access it you need a Premium subscription of around £30 a month, and you can start with a free month-long trial.

Workshops and masterclasses are often just a one-day commitment, making them a quick and highly practical way to throw yourself into action and experience what something is really all about. You can find workshops all over the place. Check out the events or outreach programmes of museums, organizations and industry bodies that interest you or hop over to some of these websites:

- https://howtoacademy.com/
- https://www.theguardian.com/guardian-masterclasses
- https://www.eventbrite.co.uk/

Dave paid just £12.99 for a course on Udemy when he was investigating his move out of the travel industry and into programming.

'I would come home every evening from work, put the kids to bed at seven, eight o'clock. And then I would just take my laptop and go and sit in the spare room and study for hours. And although it was hard, I did genuinely enjoy the studying and it really did go through my head, wow, if I could do this as my job that would be fantastic. I tried and tested it by doing those courses and thinking yeah, this is what I want to do. And I did it over a long enough time and didn't get bored of it to be sure it was sustainable.'

TIP: Learning is Not a Passive Experience

It's not just what you are being taught that's valuable here. Doing any form of Lean Learning also brings you into contact with other people (seeing a theme here?), be they kindred spirits on the course with you or the expert teaching staff. Online courses in particular increasingly have some kind of community element – a Facebook group or online portal where you can open discussions and seek advice. Make a point of asking questions of the tutor, chatting to your fellow students and arranging to keep in touch – it can open you up to a wealth of information, new resources and helpful pointers on where else to explore. You may even build a new mini community to partner you along your journey. Your new networks of support will be important on this expedition.

3. Industry Immersion

Another key element of your research is to actively immerse yourself in the world of your Future Me. Set out to get familiar with the trends, challenges, language, key concepts and important players in that alternative universe and feel what it would be like to live as a native. Then see if you like it, if it feels like 'you' and whether it still interests and motivates you.

Don't let the word industry mislead you. The kind of activities I'm suggesting work just as well whether you hanker for big pharma or furniture making.

There are of course some decent passive ways of doing this too – subscribing to a specialist website or publication, becoming a member of an industry body, keeping across any relevant articles, following key thought leaders on Twitter or joining a LinkedIn Interest group. All of those will grow your knowledge. But those should only be the first level of immersion, because I also want you to *do stuff*. Because *doing stuff* is a level of commitment that brings much greater results.

Commit to going to places and events – where the people you want to be hang out, where the industry you need to know about gets discussed, where the concepts that excite your Future Me are explored.

You'll find plenty of ways of doing this: look out for conferences, trade fairs or shows, lectures and book launches.

Joining LinkedIn and Facebook groups will also help you hear about upcoming events. See the Resources section at the back of the book to find out how to do this.

Meet Up is another useful resource. It's a website that allows you to find and join groups related to your interests: https://www.meetup.com/

TIP: Opportunities Are on Your Doorstep

The events you attend needn't be grand affairs. Indeed, starting local can feel far more manageable and help you build your confidence before moving further out of your comfort zone. If your Future Me is running her own craft business, you don't have to book expensive tickets to the Spirit of Christmas fair in London. Heading to the local craft fair to chat to the artists working successfully in your area is a great start and gives you the ease of places and possibly even people in common. Keep an eye on the events section of your local community or newspaper website. Once you start actively looking, you'll be amazed at the amount going on in your own town that you were not even aware of. In your career change journey, starting small and working upwards is a useful guiding principle.

4. Walking the Walk

How do you find a way to do the job of your Future Me before you're really doing the job? This next form of research means road-testing the day-to-day reality of the work you're envisaging so you can experience it first-hand.

We're all familiar with the concept of work experience from our children or from our own teen years. If your 16-year-old daughter declared she wanted to be a lawyer based on nothing but an obsession with Netflix crime dramas, you and her school would encourage her to go and spend some time at the local court or a few days with the local solicitor experiencing what lawyers actually do day to day. How can you know if you'll like something if you only have your own imagination to go on? So let's find your Future Me a 'work placement'.

Volunteering

Volunteering is a fantastic way to dip a toe into a new industry, sector or role that you're curious about. If volunteering only conjures images of a long-ago gap year under foreign skies or sheepishly petitioning local businesses for school raffle prizes, you're missing a trick. Used *strategically*, volunteering can be a powerful weapon in your career redesign armoury. The key is asking not only 'What can I *give*?' but also 'What can I *get*?'

'Strategic volunteering' is all about giving back whilst also using and developing your skills, gaining valuable experience, knowledge and contacts.

Naturally, the majority of traditional volunteering opportunities fall in the charity sector. Now you may not want to work in that sector but – approached strategically – you can still test your ideas here. The key is to select opportunities that match the role you want to test, not where you're just an extra pair of hands. Many websites now have a filter you can apply to narrow the kind of volunteer roles you're after, e.g., marketing, teaching, catering, finance, comms, tech.

But aside from the charity sector, formal and informal volunteering opportunities are everywhere and there's nothing to stop you offering your services to anyone! Who doesn't want a helping hand? Events can be a great place to volunteer – a book, film, food or music festival, a wedding fair, sports event, business conference . . . whatever sets your heart racing and helps you to build your knowledge, contacts and first-hand experience.

Make a list of target organizations in the sector that you're passionate about – mind mapping (see Chapter 7) can be useful here. If culture and heritage are your thing, try approaching your local National Trust property, theatre, gallery, garden or museum. Don't just google volunteer roles and give up if there are none currently available. Search your Circle of Connections for links to businesses or friends of friends. Identify key people and make them an offer of help. It can be powerful to be specific about *how* you can be useful. Often this might initially be based on your current skills – if you're a digital marketing specialist who wants to move into arts events management, why not offer to work on the local theatre's Instagram account for a month? Dealing with the events manager, you'll soon get a flavour of what that job entails.

Get ready to ask lots of questions and build a clearer picture of the organization or profession to see if it really is what you're imagining.

Another interesting volunteering avenue for career changers looking to investigate a new sector, expand their network, differentiate themselves on a CV or take on a more senior role can be to take on a non-executive director (NED) position.

If that sounds overly formal and has you thinking of City boardrooms and smart suits, think again. 'Boards of directors' in whatever guise exist everywhere from your local museum, theatre or football club to hospitals, universities, private companies and charities. Approached strategically, any of the following kinds of voluntary role could be helpful in exploring your Future Me. Try some of these organizations:

To take your skills on to a board or work as a charity trustee:

- https://www.gettingonboard.org/
- https://www.womenonboards.net/en-gb/home.aspx
- https://reachvolunteering.org.uk/

To be a school governor:

- https://www.inspiringgovernance.org/volunteers/
- https://www.nga.org.uk/Governance-Recruitment/ Be-a-school-governor-or-trustee.aspx

To work as a magistrate:

- https://www.gov.uk/become-magistrate/apply-to-be- a-magistrate

These are likely to be longer-term voluntary commitments but are great options for building your connections in a new arena, establishing your credibility, gaining new skills, proving your leadership capabilities, helping you understand how certain bodies are managed and run, or growing your confidence after some time out of formal work.

Shadowing

Spending real time – be that a day or a week – with someone who does the work that's calling to you is ideal. Classic work experience territory. Again, your Circle of Connections is a great place to start looking for shadowing opportunities. Friends of friends are far more likely to agree. If appropriate, consider building on a really successful Curious Conversation with a request to spend some time with that person. If you can't find a link to the person you'd really love to shadow, try offering an exchange. Currently working as an accountant but have a wedding photographer as a Future Me? Ask for a day shadowing your local wedding photographer in exchange for half a day's help on their tax return!

Sometimes shadowing can be the start of something far more concrete, as Anthea, 50, discovered when she called up her local undertaker wondering if she could take her building project management skills in a new direction:

'I literally googled the nearest funeral directors to my house, called them and offered my time for free because I knew nothing about funerals. The woman I spoke to said, "Yes, we always need a bit of help. You're welcome to come in." The funeral director asked if I'd ever seen a dead body before and I said only my granny when I was ten. He showed me a lady in the Chapel of Rest. It was a bit of a test. And I was fine about it. I really was quite surprised at myself. He showed me around then, and it's a small independent funeral directors, doing everything from collecting to the funeral and beyond, gravestones and everything. And he said, "Would you like to come in tomorrow and spend the day? Because it's a funny job and it's not really for everybody." And I came on that Thursday and I never left!'

There's more on what took Anthea from project manager to funeral director on page 282.

Mini Projects

Mini projects are the perfect way to see if a Future Me is as fun as you think. How can you run your own cafe if you've never made a cappuccino? Give up your Saturdays to work for a caterer or in the restaurant down the road.

Get your imagination to work on how to use some of your spare time doing the work of your Future Me.

It might sound obvious, but if you think you might want to be a website designer, you need to design a website. Who do you know who is setting up their own business and needs a virtual shopfront? Maths Tutor Future Me really needs to tutor someone. So find two mates with primary school-aged children and offer some lessons or arrange to run an after-school club. Want to be a professional declutterer? Identify a friend with a house in chaos and give up a Saturday to test your inner Marie Kondo. Wonder if Personal Stylist Future Me could really work? Arrange a shopping trip for your three friends who never get out of sweatpants and find out.

Janette, who is now selling her own furniture creations after twenty years in the police force, certainly got stuck into a bit of trial and error. Her full journey is on page 309.

'I had literally just painted my kitchen – that was a lockdown project – and then, after a glass or two of Prosecco, I told my husband I was going to paint a sideboard! So I bought one for about £40 off Marketplace and I sold it to a couple in the West Country six weeks later for £500. By the time I'd got home (I forgot to factor in delivery!), they'd emailed me to say they wanted another one. I did a few more pieces. I think I did about seven or eight and they all sold within two weeks.'

Mini projects work extremely well if your Future Me is an extension of a hobby or skill set you are already developing and are considering using professionally. Perhaps you're on the cusp of a so-called side hustle. If so, you're probably wondering if there is a market, whether it would make money and whether you'd really enjoy it. Stop wondering and *do* something. Before you start mentally designing your business cards, find short sharp ways to see if you (and other people!) actually have a real appetite for the service or product you want to offer.

TIPS: Getting into Action on a Mini Project

Mini projects should ideally be small, simple and reasonably fast ways to explore the world of your Future Me and see if it matches the vision you have. Choose something that you can start straightaway and which doesn't require a huge amount of preparation. Perfectionism is a classic cause of procrastination.

Involving someone else as a guinea pig or paying client will give you accountability to ensure you really do it and give you valuable feedback on the viability of your idea.

Don't overlook opportunities to try on your Future Me within your current job. Stick your hand up for a short-term project on another team or in another department more aligned to your new career idea. Spot a gap you could fill, ask to go on a particular training course or attend a conference. Set up a lunchtime club, a volunteering project or charity venture that allows you to investigate your alternative self.

I have a confession to make. Many years ago, I spent a lot of time daydreaming about linocut cards and prints. I had a beautiful website in my head and visions of craft fairs and trade shows. Alongside my BBC work, I was doing an enjoyable printmaking course at my local FE college. It wasn't until I paid for a day-long workshop at the V&A Museum in London aimed at card and print designers wanting to grow their business, that I realized something rather embarrassing. The other people on the course were serious. They were ploughing a lot of energy into creating and selling and grafting. I sat there and realized how ridiculous it was that I was keen to grow a business I hadn't even attempted to start! I rarely made any prints outside of course hours. I was in love with the idea but not the reality. If I loved making prints, I would be making prints. I wasn't walking the walk, just dreaming a dream. Now I'm running my own coaching business, I've ticked that entrepreneurial box. But I was definitely barking up the wrong tree in the art world.

Key Takeaways

You can't simply think your way into a convincing career decision. You need to do things.

Finding ways to properly investigate your Future Mes helps you make a more confident and informed choice about what is right for you.

Researching your career ideas should be a predominantly active rather than passive activity.

The magic is in the people: other people are one of the most powerful resources for a career change.

Be in explorer mode – the more open you are as you investigate, the more you will gain from the journey and the unusual twists it might take.

Now is a great time to revisit the core principles of Commitment, Curiosity and Courage from Chapter 2.

Action Checklist

- [ ] I have detailed the questions I want to answer around each of my Future Mes.

- [ ] I have built my Circle of Connections

- [ ] I am arranging Curious Conversations

- [ ] I am taking the Ten Thank You Cards Challenge

- [ ] I have found opportunities for Lean Learning

- [ ] I am undertaking Industry Immersion

- [ ] I am finding ways to Walk the Walk

This is a serious action list!

Depending on the shape of your Future Mes, this part of your career change investigation may be where you want to spend several weeks or even a number of months.

Chapter 10
Really Doing It

So the data is coming in! Your career experiments are allowing a Future Me to take shape that you are excited to commit to bringing to life.

But how? Perhaps you've been focusing on raising your children for seven years and feel anxious about how to manage that 'gap'. Or maybe everyone knows you as an HR executive and you now want to be a social media manager. Your whole network is built around finance and now you want to break into the travel industry. You want to start your own business but have only ever been an employee. Yikes, says your brain. What do I need to do next?

You need to get A from B, but this is unlikely to happen in one great leap. If this is going to be successful and have real focus and momentum, you need to identify the series of stepping stones ahead of you.

To do that, you're going to take a good, honest look at where you are now in relation to where you want to get to. Based on this assessment, you'll build a clear Action Plan to bridge that gap, guided by some important principles on goal setting.

And whilst everyone's journey is unique, I'll share with you some common foundations that career changers find helpful to put in place.

Building Your Action Plan

The first thing to do to equip you to build your plan is to step back and assess where you've got to. Reflect on what you've discovered you already have going for you and areas that need work. Identify the key milestones, big and small, that you need to reach and the things that could trip you up along the way.

You're going to do some serious SWOTting in order to design your Action Plan. Not sure what SWOTting is? Let me explain.

Businesses around the world have been using the SWOT analysis for over 50 years to identify their Strengths, Weaknesses, Opportunities and Threats so that they can shape the best strategies for moving forwards with confidence towards their ideal outcomes.

But SWOT is a great tool for your own individual career journey too. You're going to undertake your own personal analysis to generate the raw material for your Action Plan.

Based on what you've learnt from your career experiments, use the guidelines and the example table on page 195 to build your own SWOT analysis of the following four areas. It will provide lots of pointers for you to turn into actions.

Strengths

This is where you write down everything that you've discovered is already in your favour for this career move. This might include qualifications you already have, personal strengths that equip you well for the new role, evidence of relevant skills and experiences, a potential client base, contacts in the industry, savings in the bank, a supportive partner, a great mentor, the ability to take some paid leave. This is a kind of confidence bank as well as a way of spotting things you should play to, showcase, maximize or take advantage of in some way.

Weaknesses

This is where you identify anything that your Future Me research experiments have shown needs developing or reshaping to maximize your chances of success. This could include knowledge or skills gaps, a CV or social media footprint that's not telling the right story, limited connections to your new field, lack of concrete experience, a career break you are nervous about explaining, uncertainty about the market for your product or service, or limited funds.

Opportunities

Here's where you capture all the great things you've learnt about where you need to focus. You might include a list of organizations or places you'd love to target, note down trends in your chosen field that are ripe to capitalize on, problems you've spotted that you can help solve, people you've identified who may have work to offer, potential partnerships, upcoming events, jobs you've heard about, internships or perhaps returnships – short-term positions which often include training to allow women who've taken a career break to build their confidence and experience. These opportunities will guide how you move forwards.

Threats

This is where you are honest about things that might derail you moving forwards. This might be a lack of time, energy or resources, other commitments that are swamping you, people in your life who are not proving supportive, uneven division of work at home, challenges around childcare or supporting elderly relatives. Your career planning needs to be seen holistically and your Action Plan might need to be backed up by conversations at home, financial planning, things you need to say no to, and some changes to family life. Identifying threats is not a reason not to do something, but a chance to ensure you are one step ahead!

My Personal SWOT Analysis

Strengths
S

Opportunities
O

Weaknesses
W

Threats
T

Current Me

Future Me

Here's a fictional example SWOT analysis for Karen, who wants to move from French teacher to education consultant. Her long-term aim is to run her own business advising parents on school choices.

Strengths	Weaknesses	Opportunities	Threats
• Great credentials as a teacher myself • Experience getting my own children into the schools that were right for them, including SEN provision • School holidays provide some extra time for me to work on this • Have successfully run career research mini projects helping some friends with this • Network of teaching colleagues to advise me • Excellent interpersonal and research skills • French language skills could also allow me to tap into international families who are relocating • Evidence collected that a lot of parents are overwhelmed by the school system and varying entry requirements	• No social media presence or marketing experience • Knowledge currently focused mostly on west and north London only	• Potential to go part-time in current teaching job or investigate supply roles • Existing local education consultant firm may be looking for associates in the summer • Links with parents could help me find clients • This could be done 1-2-1 or initially via some group workshops • Sister has 9-year-old and a network of parents with children approaching senior school • Develop links with the French primary schools where we have our existing classmate 'twinning' scheme • Curious Conversation with friend Sarah suggests opportunity to partner with her local estate agency • Brother-in-law Steve has designed his own website and could help me design mine	• Current job has security and pension • Seasonal nature of the work, heavy over summer and New Year, but quieter in spring • No childcare of my own over the summer months

Undertake your own SWOT analysis like Karen's using the blank template below. Create a beautiful brain dump about your situation. It will reflect how well equipped you feel and where there is work to be done.

Strengths	Weaknesses	Opportunities	Threats

Look at what you've written and pull out any observations that now need translating into action. These will form the basis of a clear plan you'll design to guide your journey forwards.

In Karen's case, for example, she's become aware through her assessment of her weaknesses that she needs to build a social media presence and she wants to get some marketing experience. She has the opportunity to potentially go part-time in her teaching role and is aware of a local consultancy firm that might offer her summer work. And so on . . .

These realizations all have actions attached and yours will too. Whether it's conversations you need to have, meetings you need to arrange, training you want to undertake, an application you need to put together, documents to collate, information you need to gather or a CV you need to rewrite, all these steps need to be captured on your Action Plan.

To help you do that effectively, be guided by these well-established principles of effective goal setting . . .

Setting Smart Goals

To make sure your action goals are clear and reachable, each one should be:

Specific

Write out *exactly* what each step you are planning involves and always use a verb to take ownership of the action.

So not some vague goal like 'Course' or 'CV' but 'Identify and sign up for three-month course which costs less than £500' or 'Arrange three sessions with my old colleague Mark about how to improve my CV to highlight my relevant skills and explain my career shift'.

Measurable

Open outcomes leave you floundering and unable to see if you've successfully completed a task and are ready to move on.

So instead of setting a goal to 'Improve my accounting skills' or 'Find more reflexology clients to practise on', make those outcomes measurable: 'Become fully competent in double-entry system and reading a balance sheet' and 'Sign up five new practice reflexology clients over the next two months'.

Achievable

Everyone's time and resources are different. If you find yourself setting goals that feel too big and unwieldy, break them down into smaller steps. Expecting yourself to tackle massive steps too fast will kill your motivation and self-belief.

Relevant

Beware of shiny object syndrome! It's easy to get derailed and lose sight of the big picture if you allow yourself to always get distracted by the newer, more fun tasks. This regularly shows up for career changers planning to set up their own business. It's the part of you that can waste days choosing fonts or getting the perfect photo for your website, instead of finding an actual client or visiting the bank to find out about extending your overdraft. Sort your goals according to how genuinely relevant they are to making progress.

Time-based

Goals with no date attached are quick to drift. As you build your Action Plan, integrate a timescale. Consider when you would ideally like to have fully stepped into your Future Me and work backwards from there to the present day, whether those actions are spread over six months or two years.

Then make use of your diary to schedule the tasks that will ensure you keep moving towards your targets: what day and time are you going to take a particular action? How long do you need? This ensures you protect these activities from other demands on your time. The challenge of a career change is that it can often feel hugely important but not urgent, so it's always under assault from more immediately pressing things.

Here's how Karen's Action Plan might look once she's SMARTened it up:

Timing	Smart Goal
Every week from now on	*Schedule two hours a week to actively research schools in south and east London, as well as boarding schools in the commuter belt* *Research to include reading inspection reports, conversations with existing parents and staff, school Open Day visits*
Every month from now on	*Work with two pro bono clients and attend one in-person or online school industry event*
By 10 September	*Arrange meeting with MyHouse estate agents. Start to identify and approach other local agents and relocation firms*
By 17 September	*Arrange meeting with Celine Lesbirel at French school. Seek out links to American and German schools*
By October half term	*Speak to Head about potential to go part time after Easter*
By 31 October	*Get totally clear on current school pension arrangements and talk to Independent Financial Advisor about private pension*
By end November	*Have meetings/conversations with three supply teaching agencies*

Every Tuesday night from January	*'Online Marketing for Dummies' course at local college*
By end of February half term	*Start 'Which School?' Instagram account and post three times a week. Write five-page guide to choosing the right school for your child*
By end March	*Have basic three-page website built with Steve's help. Have contributed two articles on choosing schools to local family/parent websites/magazines and been on two podcasts aimed at parents*
By end April	*Trial 'Choose the Right Secondary School' workshop for parents at own school*
By end May	*Arrange meeting with John at local education consultants to revisit ad hoc work opportunities*
By mid June	*Have professional childcare in place for two days a week and a one-day-a-fortnight informal arrangement with granny/friends ready for the summer holidays. Have two group 'Choose the Right School' workshops in place for ten parents from other schools, including niece's*
By mid July	*Have four paying clients to work with 1-2-1*
By next September	*Have mix of part-time teaching and education consultancy work, with supply work if needed*
By following Easter	*Be working fully on education consultancy work with domestic and international client base*

Naturally, your Action Plan will flex and evolve as you go along, so revisit it regularly, ideally at the start of each week, to make detailed and practical updates, additions or revisions. That way you will stay focused, clear on where you are going and committed to staying on track towards your goals. Start now.

Timing	Smart Goal

Building on Firm Foundations

Whilst no two career changes are exactly the same, it's likely that your Action Plan will take you into some common career-change territory. As you get started on planning your journey, I want to talk you through some potential pitfalls, regular sticking points, unusual challenges and useful strategies. Let me kick off with some reflections from my personal experience before outlining six helpful foundational principles.

In my own 18-month transition from BBC news presenter to fully-fledged career coach, I had my fair share of wobbly moments and practical hurdles. Twenty years with an internationally recognized broadcaster had given me a professional credibility and at times it felt mad to be leaving that behind me. It was like a protective cloak I was nervous to part with. Taking real ownership of the new version of myself took time and meant I had to get my own head around it first before I felt confident to talk more widely about what I was doing. It was especially hard in the early stages, when I was very aware of what a beginner I was in the coaching field, compared to the decades of experience I had as a journalist. I didn't like that feeling much and needed to see my professional existence much more holistically in order not to feel such a novice. We'll look at the internal shift that requires.

I spent a long time tweaking and playing with my LinkedIn profile, CV and Instagram profile to explain this move I was making. I needed it to make sense to other people and I needed to be taken seriously. So messaging is important. I distinctly remember the day I finally changed my LinkedIn details to say 'former BBC journalist', typed 'coach' as my current job and pressed Save. It was both scary and exhilarating. Letting go is as much a part of a career change as stepping up.

It helped me to move gradually. I started my coaching qualification whilst I was still working as a news presenter, making time on weekends to attend training sessions and finding practice clients in my spare time. Fortunately, my freelance work patterns gave me the capacity to do this, and my salary allowed me to fund the course. I'm aware those aren't luxuries everyone has. So I'll share some thoughts on how you can best transition from one career to the next in different ways and invite you to consider how long you might need to do this and any changes or support you will need.

In my case, working as a coach also meant setting up my own business – a website, a strategy to find clients, doing my own admin, getting comfortable talking about my prices and services. One thing that helped me enormously was forging relationships with other coaches, be that online or in person, through my training cohort, local contacts or Facebook groups. I felt supported, understood and had access to practical advice from others on the same journey. Going it totally alone, particularly if your career change means working solo, can be hard. And growing a viable business takes time and energy. Find your community and keep up with the support network you identified right back in Chapter 2.

Those of you changing sector or role and looking for employment, rather than setting up on your own, have to manage the process of landing a new job. The normal application and interview process can be tricky for career changers, so I want to show you some of the approaches you should consider.

Whilst your experience will not be identical to mine and not all of the strategies that follow are relevant to every career move, they are great foundations for you to think about as you get underway. I hope that knowing that what you are encountering is neither unusual nor insurmountable, and that there are proven practical and mindset approaches you can adopt, will make all the difference.

Own Your Evolution Story

Before we even touch on the practicalities, one of the most challenging things about making a career change is reshaping and retelling your story, and doing so in a way that doesn't make you squirm with uncertainty and discomfort. You are nervous of people judging you and probably assume they wonder what the hell you are doing. Partly because you will have moments where you ask yourself the same question!

Career changers often worry that their story doesn't make sense to the outside world. But just because you started life with an accountancy degree, became a teacher and have now decided to become a florist that doesn't mean you have 'jumped around' or 'not stuck with one thing'.

Before you can confidently share your career change story, I'd suggest your evolving identity needs a bit of internal work. You need to truly understand and believe in the new version of yourself.

In fact, that inclination to think of yourself as two different people – a totally new version and an obsolete old version – can be part of the problem. It risks negating and devaluing all that's gone before and leaving you feeling exposed in a fresh new skin. But is there really an *old* you and a *new* you? Are you really starting totally afresh? I doubt it. The work you've done throughout this book should have shown you the threads that have run throughout your life that you are now stitching together to make a better fitting coat than you've ever had before. This is still the *same* you, experienced, skilled and valuable, simply evolving naturally in a new direction.

Sam, who now works for a charity after being a teacher for some two decades, initially struggled to get to grips with her supposed 'new' identity.

'Actually, it was a couple of friends, and my husband too, who reminded me: "A teacher isn't what you are. You are all those other things. Teacher is just what you used to do." And

I had to change that mentality to say what I was doing is not who I am. And I'm really happy with it now. I'm Sam and I work at the Co-op and I love it. It was just so enlightening. It's lovely to realize that there are other things out there and that gave me confidence again, which I needed.'

Freddie, actor-turned-nurse in his thirties, has some great insights on the mindset that worked for him.

'When people ask me about leaving acting, I say it's still a love for me and something that I carry with me. I'm not a different person now. And it's not like I don't want to talk about the last ten years, but I'm doing this now because this is going to give me, I hope, a richer future. So it's owning it. And you don't have to explain it to anyone, but you also shouldn't hide it away because it's part of what's pushing you towards something else.

'A career change is a bit like when a relationship ends – I think the worst thing people can say to you is "That's the best thing that could have happened" or "I never liked them anyway" or "You're so much better without them". Because that can invalidate months, years, whatever time, emotional energy and growth that they've put into their relationship or career, it invalidates all of that in a swoop. Every part of your career is part of your history. We can take it with us if we need to, or we can put it down when it serves.'

Remember you can hear more about the thoughts that go through the minds of career changers like you in Chapter 12.

Have you started to see a coherent narrative in your career journey? Can you pinpoint your personal brand throughout the twists and turns? Can you express who you are and the consistent driving forces in your professional life?

One of the things that helped my internal ownership of my move from journalist to career coach was to stay focused on the recurring themes in my life that had led me to where I was.

I think of it as looking at your career patchwork and spotting the common threads that pull it all together.

Try building a timeline of the significant periods in your life to date. You might want as many as ten or fifteen. Include hobbies and passions, important trips you've made or courses you took and loved. Powerful events in your personal life. Look for your common themes and see how they help you make sense of your evolving story and really own what has brought you to this point.

Here's my very rough career timeline from university to now with the consistent themes I have come to recognize underneath. You might start with your childhood or schooldays. For clarity, I've stuck to headlines but you can scribble down more details on yours for however many stages of your life jump at you as being significant in bringing you to this point.

Threads in Your Career Patchwork

Degree in modern languages

Year abroad teaching

Join MI6??

BBC news presenter

Personal development and career coach

Student theatre

BBC reporter and producer

Facilitator, event chair, podcaster

Communicator • Questioner • Truth-seeker • Interpreter
Listener • Educator • Performer • Story-teller • Champion

So, let me return in a little more detail to the overview of my own career story that I gave you way back in the Introduction to help explain my timeline and what I mean by common threads.

I did a modern languages degree (French, German, Italian – thanks for asking) at university with a year spent teaching in Vienna. I was heavily involved in student theatre.

After graduating, I toyed with lots of career ideas: actress, the Foreign Office, charity or arts administrator, spy (yes, really, I was approached by MI6), journalist.

I plumped for the latter, got a postgraduate journalism qualification under my belt and joined the BBC in Newcastle as a radio reporter. BBC Radio 4 (consumer and women's affairs) and presenting on the BBC News Channel followed. So did some event chairing and podcast interviewing.

Along the way I had two year-long career breaks when our daughters were born.

After almost two decades at the BBC, I trained and qualified as a personal development and career coach, specializing in supporting women.

On the surface of it, there are bits that might seem 'higgledy'. How does a would-be actress end up as a radio reporter? Why does that journalist become a career coach? But actually, when you look at the powerful describing words underneath, it makes total sense to me. They are my common threads and my driving forces.

I love to communicate, investigate, teach, question, perform, listen, champion people's stories, delve for the truth and bring clarity.

These are the powerful stitches that pull my career together and they show up in all the significant things I have done academically, personally and professionally to arrive where I am today. They are words that can be applied to all my roles, from modern languages student and overseas teacher through my love of acting in my spare time, to my career journey from reporter and presenter to coach and the event facilitation work I still enjoy doing. They have simply shown up and evolved in different ways.

I have a deep belief in the logical connection between my work at the BBC and what I do now and find it much easier to explain, having got curious about the common threads in my life. Underpinning both my journalism and my coaching are the deep listening, expert questioning and analytical skills vital to get to the heart of people's complex stories and to create challenge and, ultimately, change.

When you have drawn a timeline of your own, spend some time looking for your common threads. What words pull together the significant times of your life, both professionally and personally? Those words might be centred on skills, people, interests, places, activities or even feelings. See what connections you can make between the various stages. What are the consistent themes that have always been stitched into your life and that you are still drawing on now as you plan your next move? It's these threads that can help you create a narrative around your evolving career.

Did I actually join MI6? It's work that certainly fits with some of my narrative themes. I remember them seeing in my 21-year-old self the potential to be a powerful listener, a skilled communicator, good at building relationships and understanding people's motivations. All vital for someone recruiting and running agents. I could tell you if I went ahead. But then I'd have to kill you . . . and where would that leave your career move?

But seriously, it's an interesting moment to reflect on . . .

I actually withdrew before the final round of tests and interviews. Why? The intellectual challenge and the thought of working to potentially combat terrorism and international crime did appeal to my desire to effect positive change. I would certainly get to investigate, question and listen. But I had a strong instinctive feeling that it wasn't right for me. Which I now know was my gut brain. I was uncomfortable about the inevitable secrecy required, which I now see goes against my desire to communicate, perform and share! I was sceptical about whether I would always be able to champion the needs of everyday people in the face of politics and whether the truth and honesty that I expect from others would always be what we were aiming for.

Twenty-five years on, my decision makes perfect sense. It just wasn't the real me.

Transmit the New Message

Whilst that process of fully inhabiting this evolving version of yourself takes place internally, there's a significant need for you to operate convincingly on an external level too. To have a career evolution story that works persuasively and that makes sense to other people. If they are going to help you or take you on, they will want and need to *understand* the change you are making and your first job is to make that easy for them.

The career threads that you have discovered will definitely help you weave your story together in your own head and in casual conversation. But when people encounter you on paper and online, will they find a clear message? You are essentially rebranding yourself. If you are telling conflicting stories about who you are, other people will be muddled too and could be less likely to buy into you as a result.

What would people think and assume about you and the work you want to do if they were to look at all the readily available public information? Consider how you want to take control of that narrative and gently reshape the footprint you currently leave.

Social Media Audit

Take a look at your online presence and see what story it tells to people who look you up (which they inevitably will do). If you are publicly active, do you post, share and comment on topics firmly linked to where you want to be rather than where you are or where you used to be? Are you following key players and organizations in your new field? Are you highlighting any work (paid or otherwise) or activities that tell your new story? Do you have a presence that provides convincing evidence for the direction you are heading in? If that is going to be a creative or entrepreneurial venture away from your current profession, is it time to start building a digital trail that tells that story too?

Professional Profile

If you are on LinkedIn (and I strongly recommend you should be), look at your profile and the impression it gives. Minimize the focus on your current role or organization if it is very different from where you are heading and draw attention to your relevant transferable skills instead. It can be horribly unhelpful to have a profile that screams marketing manager if you want people to see you as a would-be graphic designer.

Here are ten key pointers on how to get your career change messaging right on LinkedIn. It goes without saying that any changes you make should be a fair and honest reflection of your situation – no porkies!

1. Think about the visuals – ensure you use a photo that gives the right impression for the industry you are looking to head into. If your photo currently looks

pretty formal and 'officey', it might need changing if your target organizations are creative and casual, or vice versa. The larger background photo, which many people leave on the default setting of somewhat bland swirls, can be an opportunity to strengthen the new story you want to convey. Could there be a stronger visual for you here which makes it clear you are all about garden design, travel, libraries, healthcare, charities, etc.? That might be a photo of a project you've undertaken, a conference you've attended, a volunteering picture, or something from the portfolio of work you've done for friends. Of course the picture should look professional, but it can allow for some individuality.

2. Make use of your 220-character Headline to share your future direction. Don't waste space simply naming your current or most recent job and telling the wrong story. So instead of 'PA, ABC Widgets' try something more open such as 'Experienced office manager seeking position in arts administration'. If discretion about your move is needed with your current employer, compromise on 'Experienced office manager and events organizer', pushing to the fore elements of your work that will tick boxes in your desired next role.

3. If you wish, you can uncheck the box that defaults to showing your Current Position in your intro, so you can minimize the immediate focus on where you are based at the moment.

4. You are asked to select an Industry. This information is not displayed on your profile but helps recruiters and other people find you in keyword searches. So consider choosing the industry you want to move into rather than your current industry.

5. Your About section offers you 2600 marvellous characters (or 370 words) to really position yourself and guide the reader to where you are going, rather than where you've been. Don't use this to talk through your job history to date, which will throw potential employers off the scent! Instead, make it your mission to demonstrate the transferable skills you have that work for your new career. Feel free to talk about recent voluntary work, training, qualifications or particular projects that show where your emphasis is now and to evidence your relevant experience. Use job ads and profiles from people in your target field to spot the key skills you should try to show and mirror the industry language you need.

6. Your Experience section may appear to be a simple work history, but it's still yours to shape as you wish. Once again, don't be shy to frontload recent voluntary, freelance or short projects you have undertaken related to the move you are planning. When describing your previous roles, think about how you can draw out the transferable elements and steer clear of language and jargon that keeps you stuck in your previous world. Emphasize specific tasks or responsibilities that equate in any way to the needs of your next employer.

7. Your Education section is a good place to mention any training – big or small – that relates to your career change. You can rework the order, so that your evening class certification in Event Management hits the eye before your ancient degree in Biology.

8. The Skills section is another area that is used by the internal search function to get you in front of the right employers. You can list up to 50 skills, but that's

probably overkill. Between 15 and 30 will do just fine. If you have an existing profile, cull or tweak any skills that don't have any relevance to your next chapter. You can choose slightly more generic descriptions – in my case, with a move from journalism to coaching, choosing skills such as communication, public speaking and interviewing over news writing and broadcast journalism demonstrates the same talents in a less niche way. Remember you can also ask people to endorse your skills.

9. If you have Recommendations from colleagues that feel out of kilter with where you are heading, delete them or ask them to rewrite them focusing on the particular skills you've identified as important to your next steps. If relevant, seek one or two recommendations from people you have worked with in a voluntary or pro bono capacity as part of trying on your Future Me.

10. Interests – round your profile off by showing your enthusiasm and commitment to your next move. You may not have much direct experience in your chosen sector, so demonstrate your interest via the influencers and companies you follow or the groups you belong to.

CV

A standard CV is heavily weighted towards your chronological work history, drawing attention to your most recent roles. As a career changer, this format can be a killer, as it tells the wrong story, hitting potential employers straight in the eyes with a job record that may have little to do with the work you want. Never expect them to infer all the brilliant reasons you are equipped to make the shift. Just as with your LinkedIn profile, it's your responsibility to join the dots for people and make it clear how your previous work connects to your new career choice.

Rather than using a standard chronology-focused CV, consider a well-crafted profile-led CV. This will allow you to frontload your new story and give an explanation of why you are suited to the career you aspire to rather than pigeon-holing you in your current or most recent job. The overall aim is to put the greatest focus on your relevant skills rather than your now somewhat misleading work history and to push your work record slightly further down the document. This kind of CV is also useful if you've taken a career break, as it makes any time away from paid work less obvious and highlights the value you bring rather than the years you have put in.

Take a look at this example for a fictional career changer, Chrissy. Let's say Chrissy works as a sales manager in retail but wants to use her more recently gained skills and experience to apply for a job she's seen as a web designer for women's brands. She has some relevant qualifications from classes in her own time and a small portfolio of design work from a number of websites she's built for local businesses. She's also done some voluntary work helping her daughter's nursery with their online presence and communications strategy.

Chrissy Changemaker
Flat 2, Change Villas, Changetown, CH1 2XZ

T: 07511 111777 | E: ccareerchanger@work.com | Linkedin.com/in/chrissychangemaker

1

A self-starting web designer with assured technical and design skills. Proven track record of delivering visually compelling websites with great functionality, delivered on time and to client's bespoke specifications. Demonstrable understanding of branding and sales strategies and a passion for outstanding customer service from a background in women's fashion and homeware retail. Now seeking an opportunity to combine my growing web design portfolio with my considerable retail expertise at a dynamic design agency serving female-focused brands.

- *Technical expertise* – experience with InDesign, Illustrator and Photoshop, a sound understanding of both UX and UI and SEO optimization.

- *Creativity* – ranging from website design for female service-based businesses across Changetown to creating and editing social media content for expanding childcare centre @ladybirdkidz and designing innovative merchandise displays in my time as a fashion store manager.

- *Client management* – website clients praise my 'brilliant ability to listen to and interpret our brand vision' and value 'the excellent regular communication to ensure the project was on track and developing as envisaged'. I was awarded regional prize for customer service from Changecounty Fashions for outstanding interpersonal skills and ability to work under pressure.

- *Strong organizational and time management skills* – I gained web design qualifications and built and maintained numerous websites for local businesses, whilst also working in a leadership position in the retail sector and raising a toddler.

(2)

③

CAREER HISTORY

Freelance Web Designer   **2022 to present**
Creating and maintaining websites for female-led small businesses in the health and wellness sector

- Created bespoke, visually compelling sites on a variety of platforms including Godaddy, Wix and Wordpress after detailed and dynamic concept discussions with clients.

- Assisted with logo, branding and photography design.

- Modified and debugged existing sites to modernize aesthetics, functionality and responsiveness. Increased UX scores by an average of 30%.

- Optimized SEO to generate improved Google rankings, impressions and click-through rates. Conversion rates rose by an average of 23% over 3 months.

- Consistently worked to budget and schedule, often under time pressure to meet product launch deadlines.

Volunteer Social Media Manager,   **2021 to present**
Ladybird Children's Centre
Providing technical and design support to leadership team on a pro bono basis

- Established visually coherent Facebook and Instagram pages with clear content strategy resulting in a more positive impression and increased engagement.

- Maintained and updated website, successfully resolving

parents' concerns around poor communication from nursery management.

• Developed and managed a monthly newsletter using Mailchimp, which improved parent attendance at events by 20%.

Assistant Retail Manager,   **2015 to present**
Changetown Fashions
Managing a team of eight staff to deliver year-on-year sales growth and increased customer satisfaction aided by my strong creative visual merchandising strategy and my determination to communicate a youthful but high-quality brand.

• Recruited, trained and developed employees to create a highly efficient, friendly and customer-focused team with lower-than-average absence levels.

• Introduced new customer service desk and dedicated customer helpline to ensure exceptional client relationships.

• Oversaw implementation and maintenance of visual merchandising specific to Changetown Fashion corporate standards.

• Liaised with external marketing agency to oversee update of website and social media platforms, leading to greater brand recognition.

• Instigated 'Women's Wellbeing' programme of talks for female staff across the region, resulting in improved levels of morale reported at annual staff reviews.

Retail Assistant,   **2010 to 2015**
Changetown Homewares

Providing outstanding service and expert product knowledge as part of an innovative and creative five-person sales team, demonstrating strong powers of communication and persuasion.

• Assisted on average 20 customers daily in finding homeware products most suitable to their style preferences, budget and practical requirements.

• Developed a bespoke personal shopping service to increase sales by c10% annually.

• Channelled strong design abilities into in-house advertising campaigns, weekly window display changes and strong seasonal themes throughout the store.

• Instigated regular monthly feature in local online newspaper providing home décor and styling advice to coincide with in-store promotions.

EDUCATION AND QUALIFICATIONS

Web development: HTML5 & CSS Stage 2, ULearn, 2021
Photoshop, InDesign & Illustrator Level 5, Changetown Adult Community College, 2020
BTEC National Diplomas in Fashion Business and Retail
A-Levels: Art, Business Studies, French

INTERESTS/VOLUNTARY WORK (5)

Art: regular participant in life drawing classes and
workshops
Photography: picture editor for local school's
Leavers' Yearbook
Dressing Volunteer, Smartworks: equipping women with
new clothes and confidence as they prepare for interview
after an extended career break

Refer to the numbers on Chrissy's CV to see the approach I'm
recommending and what you should be thinking about as you
write your own.

(1) Start Your CV with a Profile

You will want to invest real time here. It's probably the most challenging paragraph you'll have to write! A profile is your chance
to position yourself as a relevant candidate by giving a punchy
overview of the key factors that make you a great fit.

In a few lines you are aiming to distil who you are, the core
skills and value you bring and where you are heading, rather
than where you have been. Communicate who you are with
confidence, clarity and authenticity, briefly spelling out the
connections in your career story that might not be immediately obvious. As with all things in your CV, this may need to
be tweaked each time you apply for a job to ensure you have
properly tailored it to what they are looking for.

Far too many people start with irrelevant information which
causes confusion to the reader and presents a weak case with
muddled messaging. In Chrissy's case, were she applying for

another job in retail, the opening line of her profile would likely read as follows: 'Customer-focused retail manager with over a decade's experience driving strong sales in the fashion and homeware sectors.'

You can immediately see that if she opens that way, a potential employer would wonder what on earth she is doing applying for a job as a web designer! So Chrissy draws instead on her recently acquired web skills and experience. She is careful to show confidence and competence but not over-egg her experience, and she uses both paid and voluntary experience to position herself.

Here and throughout your CV you should aim to match or echo the language, key requirements and tone of the job advert.

(2) Create a Key Skills Section

You don't have to use this technique, but adding a short section of key skills with bullet points can also help clearly show what a great match you are for the role. You can head it Key Skills or just let it flow naturally on from your profile. This section should be informed by four or five vital requirements from the job description and you should give short, proven highlights of how you meet them. This allows you to seamlessly blend examples from across your career, voluntary work and hobbies and escape the straitjacket of the more traditional CV format. Chrissy has even woven in some customer testimonials to back up what she's saying.

(3) Career History

I suggest calling this section Career History, rather than Employment History, as it gets you over the hump of thinking you can only use paid work or formal jobs as your raw material.

Look carefully at what Chrissy has done. She has frontloaded the pieces of website design work (done for friends at mates' rates) and included a relevant voluntary role, allowing her current formal job in retail to slip down into third position.

Each role needs a line or two of simple explanation of what the job was followed by a number of carefully tailored bullet points giving concrete evidence that you have the skills the next job requires. It's a common mistake on CVs for people to simply list their responsibilities in this section. This should not be a description of the job you did; it's your chance to spell out the achievements you have that match what they want. Have the job description in front of you and aim to match as many requirements as possible, or as close as you can get! (Remember job descriptions are often a recruiter's rose-tinted vision of their absolute dream candidate.)

As you can see, that is relatively straightforward when Chrissy is talking about her web design work. She can use exact requirements from the job description and show obvious matches with her skill set, closely mirroring the language. CVs may well first be scanned for keywords either by a computer or a human, so it's vital you include them.

It gets harder when Chrissy moves into the territory of her retail work. On the surface it has nothing to do with web design. This is where transferable skills come into play and the idea of 'equivalence' – producing examples that match what's needed in the web designer job from within a different context. You'll notice that the achievements and attributes Chrissy draws most attention to here are not necessarily the same as those she would use for another retail job. Instead, she works hard to evidence her transferable skills that match what the web design job has asked for: strong interpersonal abilities, her track record in listening to and implementing the needs of individual customers, her solid design and creative talents, branding knowledge, leadership and teamwork, initiative, relationship building, meeting quality standards and so on. She also gives a nod to her interest in women's issues as this is relevant to her target company.

(4) Education and Qualifications

Chrissy leads with her web design courses, however modest she may feel they are. In Chrissy's case, they are recent. If you want to draw on older qualifications to tell the best story, consider leaving out dates so you are not trapped in a chronological sequence which doesn't do your story any favours.

(5) Interests/Voluntary Work

We've already spoken about the fact that voluntary work might sometimes feature in your Career History, so don't tuck it away here if it can work harder for you higher up.

You don't have to include this section, but it's worth doing if you have genuine examples that are relevant to the job and either add to your case and the image you want to portray or are sufficiently eye-catching that they will differentiate you!

Given Chrissy is applying for a web design post, it's definitely worth her mentioning her interests in art and photography, and her Smartworks volunteering is a creative endeavour that also plays nicely into the fact the job she wants is dealing with female-focused brands.

CV Rules in a Nutshell

An effective CV is neat and clean and really doesn't require photos, fancy fonts or overly busy layouts.

Chrissy's CV fits on two sides of A4 and yours should too. Recruiters spend minutes not hours looking at them and want to find the relevant information quickly and easily. Keep it succinct and clear.

Every CV you submit should be tailored for each individual role, which may involve subtle tweaks to your language and what you include in order to make you the best match.

If you are struggling to take on your next persona, look on LinkedIn to see how other people in this field describe themselves. Don't copy but aim to match the language, key vocabulary and tone. This might also involve shifting your language to reflect the industry switch – some worlds think in terms of customers and some in terms of clients; some in terms of partners, whilst others talk about stakeholders. Mirror what you find on the ad and the company's own material.

Avoid padding out your CV with bland cliches like 'I am a hard-working team player who can also work well on my own' or somewhat meaningless phrases like 'I am a confident individual who will turn their hand to every challenge, big or small'.

Your CV should not be a description of the work you have done but a chance to make a compelling case that you have the skills required for the next job. Always work closely with the job description and be rigorous in providing actual examples, not making vague claims like 'I am an effective leader with great organizational skills'. Show me, don't tell me!

Use strong action words like 'directed', 'delivered', 'managed', 'led', 'researched', 'designed', 'devised', 'implemented', 'instigated' rather than 'did', 'undertook' or 'was responsible for'.

Focus on the tangible results your work had. What quantifiable outcomes came from your actions? Think about what changed, what improved, what increased and by how much.

When you have a decent draft, give it to one of your cheerleaders to look at. Simply get them to answer these questions: What are the three strongest messages you take from this CV? What picture does it paint? How would you describe the person you are meeting here?

Once you've got it in the best shape possible, get the opinion and advice of a friend in the same industry or one of your Curious Conversation partners.

You'll find numerous reflections on the application process from people who've been through it in Chapter 12, but here are some key insights on what can work successfully. You'll see that cover letters or personal statements can also be a big help for career changers. All of these rebranding approaches can make a huge difference in easing your journey forwards. But you need to work hard to package them up and tie them with a different bow.

Dave, who moved from the travel sector to work as a programmer:

'I remodelled my CV by putting myself in a programmer's head. I was very waffly in my old CV with big paragraphs of flowery language. But I made my new CV very concise and clear and presented it in a professional way, making sure I showed how much I knew about technology and tried to lean on my education. I've got very strong GCSEs, A-levels, a first-class degree from a good university. So I hoped they would see that they'd be getting someone who learns very well, who picks things up.

'I sent a CV out to a local firm who were looking for a junior iOS developer. They came back to me quite quickly and offered me an interview. I was worried they might laugh at me. When they asked about my experience I'd have to say, "Well, you know, I sort of sat in bed doing a course really." But the in-house recruiter said they really wanted to see me. What I didn't factor in was the emphasis they put on passion. I think they were very impressed with the fact that I'd done the course whilst working full-time in London. Their attitude was we can teach you the skills and send you on courses, we can see you're committed and that this is a massive passion for you.'

Matthew, who at 26 shifted from finance to data analysis:

'I made a one-page CV, because I'm fairly young and that is generally recommended for someone my age without a long work history. My past experience wasn't always particularly relevant, so I just had a small education and experience section and the rest was projects and skills and how those have been of value. I spelled out the relevant experience, talking about projects I'd worked on in my own time, little bits of work for companies that I'd done for free. I'd been able to find a video game company that I made something for that they found useful and I'd talked to people in specific financial firms that I was hoping to apply to and I was able to make something for them that they found interesting. I probably did four or five relatively large projects and used those on my CV.'

Victoria, who moved out of publishing and applied for nursing:

'I had to write my personal statement and I thought that meant just a paragraph. Then I started looking them up online and saw that the process was much more involved; I racked my brains about my transferable skills. I wrote about how I'm fascinated by the human body. And how I felt I was a caring person. And I thought broadly – I've run a family and I have two children who I love and look after, and my father had a stroke five years ago and I spent four months going into hospital three or four times a week to help look after him. So I'd had direct experience of what it is to help people. And I'm someone who just gets on with stuff. You know what I mean? And actually, to be a nurse, you just need to get on with stuff.'

Emily, who found the opportunity to write a personal statement made all the difference to her application to move from PR into schools admissions:

'I wrote an A4 side, explaining what I'd done and really scrutinizing the job description, pulling out the things that I could find examples of that I've done. I went over the job description many times. I used the personal statement to really develop a narrative about myself and find similarities in the roles. Yes, there were lots of differences in the jobs, but I think finding the themes and nuggets to draw on would be my advice.'

Understand Why the System is Not Your Friend

If thinking about how to make your CV tell a story that makes you a strong candidate for your new career still feels like having a bucket of cold water poured over your head, don't panic.

Wanting to make a very big shift in your work can certainly make the traditional job application process more challenging. Being one fabulously able and enthusiastic but slightly 'misfit' applicant among dozens of more conventional candidates isn't where you ideally want to be. That's not to say it never works, but it can feel like a slow and tortuous route in which your own power to influence the process is tiny and your chances of success depend on the waning imagination of a slightly frazzled recruiter or HR manager. If faced with a number of strong candidates, it's sadly predictable that they're inclined to choose the less 'risky' option of someone who's recently 'been there and done that'.

In fact, your CV may never even get in front of a living, breathing person. Many bigger companies ask for online applications and then use ATS (Applicant Tracking System) software to sift what comes in, meaning your CV may be rejected by a robot. Don't meet the strict keywords, experience or dates criteria? Computer says no.

I say all this not to discourage you but to give you some context. If a slew of rejections from the traditional application route suggests that this system isn't working well for you (and let's face it, it doesn't work well for vast numbers of people, not just career changers!) it's time for an additional approach. Because firing off endless applications into a hostile environment will exhaust your enthusiasm and confidence and cause you to assume you can't do the job.

But that's unlikely to be true. People (or computers) just don't *get* you. They can't *see* your epic potential, because all that you offer can't easily be shoehorned into an unimaginative system. Where possible, we need to get you off paper, where your story may languish unloved, and into a room with a human being, where you can make your case with real power.

By all means keep going with the traditional route once you have a great career changers CV, but don't confuse a day firing scattergun applications with a fantastic use of your time. You can spend hours sweating over a handful of applications and feel you've worked hard. But once you hit 'Send', your influence over the process is gone, with no promise of progress. You are essentially jumping up and down shouting from a vast distance . . . you need to find a way to walk over and introduce yourself!

Adopt a Different Approach

You should have your antennae tuned for opportunities that don't involve a standard application route with its photofit requirements and a stampede of candidates. You need to tap into the hidden job market.

It's hard to establish a firm figure, but estimates suggest anywhere between 30 and 60 per cent of jobs are filled without ever being formally advertised. Contrary to what you might assume, there's no legal obligation for a company to advertise a vacancy, either internally or externally. Some organizations have their own recruitment policies to adhere to, and are mindful of the need for diversity, but generally speaking they have some flexibility to freestyle. So, unsurprisingly, many bosses will look to save time and money by skipping the advertising and recruitment process and rely on their own networks and the recommendations of colleagues and staff to find a great fit. Smaller firms and start-ups without a hefty hiring budget are particularly fertile territory for hidden jobs. Bigger isn't always beautiful.

Hidden jobs include jobs that are still only a passing thought in someone's brain – a sense that in a few months they might need an extra pair of hands in the marketing department, a niggling thought that they should expand their events calendar this year or finally update their website.

Your mission is to already be on their radar when that niggle becomes a need. To be the person who springs to mind when Margaret in Accounts suddenly announces she's pregnant and will be off for 12 months. Whose name comes up in the staff meeting when there's a realization the IT system needs an overhaul.

You need to become the name at the end of this sentence: 'I know someone who could be just right . . .'

So how do you get there?

The great news is that tapping into the hidden job market is a natural extension of the work you've already embarked on during your career experimentation. I said it then and I'll say it again. The magic is in the people. Industry immersion and Curious Conversations are the perfect ways to hear about potential opportunities and to get yourself in front of people who could use your skills or recommend and connect you to others. Keep asking 'Who else . . . What else? . . . Where else?'

Continue building and nurturing those connections between yourself and the career you have in your sights. Follow up on those thank you cards to update people on the success you've had following their recommended actions. But consider taking it up a notch. When you were in the experimentation phase, the emphasis was on listening and learning. That process remains hugely valuable, but challenge yourself to go a little further.

Once you have a number of 'easy-level' conversations under your belt and have perfected your technique, it's time to move into less familiar territory and seek offers to talk to people who are a little more senior. Mention the people you've already spoken to and the actions you've been taking to demonstrate your commitment and seriousness. You should now feel able to engage in a more knowledgeable way on the issues and you might feel more confident to offer a little more about your own plans and how you see yourself fitting into the industry.

At events, start to gently up your visibility and move from listener to contributor. Ensure you ask a question or offer a thought at panel discussions. Make a point of finding and thanking the organizer. Follow up by joining the online discussion and social media coverage.

Unlocking the hidden job market is a longer investment of your time and energy, but it's potentially a far more potent one for career redesigners than joining a job board pile-on.

It was the hidden job market that worked for Clare (see page 268) as she looked to go back into marketing after a 16-year break and a detour into teaching:

'I have a very good friend who I like to go and have a cuppa with and we'd been chatting about my plans and I'd told her I was exploring going back into marketing. Then, weirdly, she just bumped into a friend of hers in the doctor's surgery of all places. The friend was going through cancer treatment and needed someone to start in the marketing department at her company in a couple of days' time and provide six months cover on a fixed-term contract. And our mutual friend said, "Well, I know somebody who wants to go back into marketing!"

'It was definitely significant that I got that work through someone I know. I realized I had actually met this lady before, so I was a slightly familiar face, and she's lovely, but the main thing was that she was prepared to take a chance on me. And when she came back after her treatment, she even asked me to stay on. She said, "What am I gonna do without my Clare?" Everyone needs a Clare, was how she put it!'

Consider Transitions as Well as Change

Have you ever noticed that all the best stories of moving between two different magical places require some kind of transition? Think Narnia and the old wardrobe packed with fur coats that the children had to pass through. Or Dorothy and her ruby slippers, without which she risked getting stuck in Oz. Lightning-scarred Harry and all those portkeys.

Now I don't recommend going and standing in a random musty cupboard looking for a magical door. But I would invite you to think about how you can best *transition* between what you are doing now and where you want to be. Whether you need to build in some time in a metaphorical wardrobe in order to shift worlds.

Career transitions can come in many forms and can help to smooth the join between what you are doing and what you really want to do. Depending on the scale of change you are making, it may feel like a stretch to simply throw in one job and start a totally different one the following Monday, though it can certainly happen. Instead, you might want to get the next role in play before you fully sever ties to the last one, or commit to an in-between step.

Think about the way you currently work. Would it help to build in a *time transition* of some kind? Read Fiona and Janette's stories in Chapter 12 to see how they are doing it – in Fiona's case over a decade!

That transition might be changing your hours or the days you work, or going from full-time to part-time to allow you a day a week to spend on building a business, doing some strategic volunteering, taking a course or working as a freelancer. Might your employer allow you some additional leave or a sabbatical? A time transition can be particularly valuable if your Future Me is looking to go it alone in some way. The portfolio career option we discussed in Chapter 5 can be used for a period of transition.

Think about where you currently work and what you do. Would a two-step *role or sector transition* be an option?

Consider this scenario. You're an accountant for a large furniture manufacturer. Your Future Me wants to be in HR for a charity. Now that involves two changes – a change of role *and* a change of sector. Making a leap that wide and that far may feel too challenging. If you're prepared to play a longer game, a more strategic approach is to change one thing at a time.

You could start with a sector transition. You take your accountancy skills into the third sector, from where you are better placed to move into HR. Meanwhile you look for opportunities inside or outside work to gain more experience and knowledge of HR to establish yourself and build your credibility.

Or you could first make the role transition. You look to move into the human resources department at the furniture company where you are already well-established, where you'll gain valuable experience in people management before applying to the charity where you really want to work. Meanwhile you could take on a volunteering role and continue with your Industry Immersion in preparation for the final push into the new sector.

Rather than try and move every piece of the puzzle at once, a two-step role or sector transition can be a more calculated approach to reach your final destination.

Another transition worth considering can be a 'foot in the door' move and several career changers featured in this book have used it with success. Just as you'd imagine, it can involve a short-term position or a slightly less-than-perfect role to help you get established. It needs careful consideration, as it can have financial or seniority implications, but see what you think.

Clare, making her return to marketing, offers this assessment of the six-month role she first took:

> 'It wasn't the best job in the world, they were a bit disor-
> ganized but it got me back in the game. The lady that I was
> working with and reporting to was just ever so slightly older
> than me, so we hit it off straightaway and she just taught
> me everything. It meant I had something recent on my CV,
> and while I was there I undertook a CRM (Customer Rela-
> tionship Management) project. Even having those three little
> letters on your CV means you've ticked another box in an
> algorithm. They didn't do a lot of modern marketing there,
> but it got me a foot in the door to the next thing – every-
> thing's a stepping stone. And I think that's another way of
> doing it – just being willing to start something and progress
> from there.'

Dave was prepared to take a programming role well below his existing status, taking a significant pay cut. Two years later, he now earns more than he did in the travel industry:

> 'Although I was a junior programmer, they never really
> saw me as a junior because I had a lot of business knowledge
> and they liked that I was more mature. It felt weird being
> at that level because I had got quite high up in my previous
> role, managing teams and things, but I viewed that first role
> as an opportunity because I think you need to get your foot
> in the door and from there you can grow.'

If you've taken a career break, there is one further transition you might consider, though not if it really holds no appeal or doesn't feel at all relevant. A short formal returnship programme (see the Resources section at the end) or a stint back in your previous career may give you the confidence boost, skills update and adrenalin hit to your CV that you need to kickstart your new professional journey, before you start your shift. Regardless of whether you choose to revisit your previous career before moving on, do at least consider revisiting old colleagues, just to remind yourself of your standing in the working world and to bring your previous achievements back to life. People are often surprised at the confidence injection that comes from picking up an old professional relationship or two and realizing they are still taken seriously and their new plans are met with genuine interest.

Be Creative in How You Fill Your Gaps

Your Action Plan may involve filling gaps you feel are going to hold you back.

How would you class these gaps – experience gaps? Credibility gaps? Skills gaps? Confidence gaps? It's good to know what you're dealing with.

Before you invest a large amount of time and money into a huge chunk of formal retraining, here are a few thoughts to consider.

Be sure your gaps are real! Feeling like you are under-equipped and being under-equipped for your career move are two different things. It's an oft-quoted statistic that men will apply for a job when they meet 60 per cent of the qualifications, women when they meet 100 per cent. The same distinction may apply to non-career-changers versus those making a shift. Consequently I've noticed that some of my clients are keen to get a new qualification to rubber stamp or authenticate their career change. Whilst that can be important in certain fields, I believe there is an inclination to want a formal certificate more for confidence than because it's really necessary.

There's no right or wrong here, but before you delay any other action steps until you have a shiny piece of paper or worry you don't have the cash to retrain, ask yourself what it is you are trying to achieve, check what evidence there is that you need to formalize this skill and consider what other ways there might be to do this. Curious Conversations will help with gathering real information on this.

Revisit 'Walking the Walk' from Chapter 9 if you have gaps to fill and consider continuing to invest time in strategic volunteering, mini projects and finding upskilling opportunities at your existing workplace.

As you actively get stuck in, you are creating the very evidence you need to overcome any perceived gaps, building new relationships and hopefully gathering recommendations and testimonials from other people.

Sometimes, as Katherine testifies, it's all about embracing the idea that it's OK to be a beginner and your skills are still valid:

'The challenge is to quiet the negative voice in your head. For example, when I tell people I am a web designer, the voice in my head asks "Are you really, if you didn't go to art school?" I have to remind myself that I know this – I may not have gone to design school, but I have studied it my whole life; I worked side by side with designers and creative directors; I am someone friends and family turn to for creative advice. I also remind myself it's not bad to be a beginner and that the idea of being a beginner is actually exciting. As a beginner your eyes are wide open; you're constantly learning and exploring new possibilities and not doing things on autopilot. And I think this can make it exciting for clients to work with you too because you're going to work harder and push yourself further to prove yourself and make them happy.'

REMINDER

Ways to Upskill Without a Full-time Course of Study

Find opportunities in your current role: apply for a secondment, ask to go on a course, volunteer for a new project or make a side move in your existing workplace.

Learn on the job: look for a position where you can gain new skills whilst you are being paid, even if it's just a transition role.

Volunteer: remember the power of strategic volunteering. Offer to help where you'll gain valuable experience and relevant new skills.

Find a mentor: who do you know from your Circle of Connections who would give you a few hours training in that computer software you're worried about or talk you through the basics of Instagram? Who is a few steps ahead of you at work and could offer you valuable information?

Use Lean Learning: online or bite-sized courses are everywhere, meaning some skills can be acquired relatively cheaply or even for free. It's amazing what you can teach yourself with a little-and-often approach.

Key Takeaways

A career change often involves a series of small steps rather than one giant leap. Thinking about a period of transition can be helpful.

It's important to know where you are starting from, where you are heading and how long you have to do it!

Career change involves telling and sharing your evolving career story – it can really help to ensure it makes sense to you before putting it out into the world.

Strong and consistent messaging about your new career direction is likely to be hugely important.

Making a change may involve some differences to the way you approach job applications and traditional routes into work, including considering the hidden job market.

Action Checklist

- [ ] I have completed my personal SWOT analysis
- [ ] I have an Action Plan with goals that are SMART
- [ ] I have a confident evolution story
- [ ] I can transmit my new message effectively (LinkedIn, CV, other relevant social media)
- [ ] I am finding ways to investigate the hidden job market
- [ ] I am exploring transition options open to me
- [ ] I am proactive and creative in filling any gaps

Step Five
Keeping Going

Chapter 11
Lasting the Course

You're on the homeward strait . . . or are you?

Actually, this is where – amid flurries of excitement and progress – you're quite likely to hit moments of feeling overwhelmed and frustrated. Where you'll sometimes take two steps forward and one step back. Where you'll get tempted to give up and head back to the known environment of your old life, however miserable.

A career redesign can take time and I want to make sure your self-belief is powered up to the max.

So this final chapter is a confidence booster. Not crass platitudes ('You go, friend!') but a deeper exploration into the way you can get your brain to work with you and not against you as you step into your redesigned life.

Understanding How Confidence is Built

Confidence is a slippery bugger. You can gain it and lose it. You can look confident without feeling it. But what is this strange substance that you sometimes have in spades and other days struggle to find? How can it be simultaneously present in one area of your life, for example, your parenting, and struggle to show up in another, your career path?

My clients often come to me at a point where they feel they've 'lost their confidence'. Taking on a career redesign, however badly wanted, can feel like a big ask.

But when it comes to making *real* progress, there is one thing I stress above all others. And it doesn't always get a great reception: Confidence comes from doing.

How many times do you find yourself thinking 'Once I feel more confident I'll write up a CV'? Or 'I need to regain my confidence before I pick up the phone to my old colleagues'?

No, no, no, no, no! Sorry, folks. Sit around waiting for the confidence fairy to pay you a visit and you risk doing absolutely nothing.

As you move forwards, I want you to remember this.

Action does not follow confidence. Confidence follows action.

It's so important, you should hear that again. Just louder.

ACTION DOES NOT FOLLOW CONFIDENCE . . . CONFIDENCE FOLLOWS ACTION.

Or as a client recently said to me in surprise, 'It's weird how once I got started, the more I do, the easier it gets.'

That's the simple way of putting it. The psychologists' explanation is the Confidence/Competence loop. Take a look . . .

The Confidence Loop

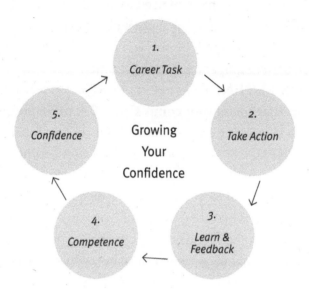

1. **CAREER TASK:** You've got your action to take. It's a bit scary. You've not tried this task before. You've not met this person, done an interview or learnt this skill. You're worried you'll be rubbish or make a fool of yourself and show what you don't know. This is where you can get stuck. And where it's tempting to sit around waiting to feel more confident. Don't.

2. **TAKE ACTION:** Start with something manageable. If the action still feels too much, break it down. Take the plunge and give it a go. Does the world fall apart? Are you so bad your friends and family stop talking to you? Does the national press camp outside your door to ask why you are an abject failure? Unlikely.

3. **LEARN & FEEDBACK:** This is where the magic starts to happen. Chances are the action goes well, or at least reasonably OK. You quickly see where there is

room for improvement. Where things weren't great, you work out what you need to do differently. Other people advise you of changes you could make. Essentially, triumph or not, you learn something and are better equipped for the next time.

4. COMPETENCE: As a result of what you learn, you start to increase your competence. You make progress, gain experience and get better. Your skill set builds.

5. CONFIDENCE: As you realize you are getting more accomplished and less fearful, so your confidence grows. As you loop around to the next action, you come at it with more self-belief. You can gradually stretch yourself to take on more challenging goals, knowing that by getting into action, you will make progress and feel more confident! Rinse and repeat.

Why Get Out of Your Comfort Zone?

You'll be aware by now that this whole journey will repeatedly require you to move out of your comfort zone in order to make progress. New territory stretches out all around you. And as we saw right back in Chapter 1, the unknown is inherently unappealing to your brain.

As a consequence, some people try to undertake a career change from within their comfort zone. The result is pretty inevitable: they quickly fall back into their default way of thinking, they use only their normal patterns of behaviour, stick to familiar environments and listen to the same small set of people. Staying in your usual bubble will have exactly the effect you imagine. You settle for the obvious. Now that's fine, if that's what all the work you've done has led you to conclude is right for you. It's not fine if you never end up making the change you really want.

Behavioural psychologists have actually identified three different operating zones, the boundaries of which are different for all of us: we each have a Comfort Zone, a Stretch or Growth Zone and a Panic or Danger Zone. No prizes for guessing where you should aim to be operating during your career change.

But it's good to understand what's going on, as you're likely to repeatedly move back and forth between all three zones on this journey. Getting attuned to what each one feels like for you will help you to course-correct.

Your Comfort Zone is not inherently bad. Starting here can be necessary to build your confidence, just as we saw with your first Curious Conversations. Your comfort zone is low on risk. Ultimately though, it's also low on reward and unlikely to allow you to realize your untapped potential. Doing what you always do will give you the results you've always got. So be honest with yourself. When you are setting goals, ask if they are a little too easy, obvious or – dare I say it – lazy. Equally, you may want to occasionally retreat here for a short while if you feel your confidence really falter. A spell back in your Comfort Zone ensures you keep moving forwards with small, manageable steps rather than suddenly stopping taking action altogether.

The Stretch or Growth Zone is considered the place of optimal performance. It's where the level of challenge we feel is, Goldilocks-style, just right to engage our creative, problem-solving brain and stimulate our growth. Too little push and we fall back into autopilot. Too much and we're soon starting to panic. Consider each of the action steps as you embark on them. A few nerves are perfectly normal and a productive amount of pressure will motivate you onwards. How do you recognize that? It's the kind of pressure that helps you perform better, that focuses your mind and ups your game. Think school – it's that tight but doable essay deadline or that all-important hockey match. Slightly nerve-racking but buzzy. And with each resulting victory we expand our Growth Zone beautifully, meaning we can attempt things that would previously have caused us stress.

The Danger or Panic Zone is when you pitch it wrong and manageable pressure becomes stress. You've moved into a space where your current skill or confidence levels don't match the complexity of the task before you. You're no longer learning, you're getting overwhelmed. Or more likely in career change terms, you're starting to feel demotivated. This isn't the moment to give up. It's about breaking down your next action into more bite-size chunks and moving back into a space which is stretching but positive.

Embracing Failure as a Learning Experience

There will be moments on this journey when you fail. I'm just coming right out and saying it. There will be jobs you don't get, opportunities that you can't land, people who tell you no.

There is a brilliant way never to fail. It's never to try anything. It works 100 per cent of the time, so feel free to adopt that method. Just don't expect any results.

Adjusting your attitude to failure is something you should do right now.

After all, I bet you're brilliant at it with your kids. It was at my daughter's primary school that I first came across the idea that FAIL stands for First Attempt In Learning.

We are happy to encourage our youngsters to get things wrong in order to move on. But so often when it happens to us, we take it personally, make assumptions about our abilities (or lack of them) and interpret it as a sign to stop.

Failure is not inherently bad. As any entrepreneur will tell you, a stack of failures can form the foundation of success, if we use them to make adjustments and build something better.

As you go through this career change process, ensure you allow yourself thinking space to learn from anything that doesn't go smoothly. Don't embed a failure as a limiting belief about yourself (see Chapter 1) but embrace it as a chance to innovate and grow.

Ask yourself:

- What was the result I wanted? How far off was I?
- What explanations were there for why that didn't work out?
- How much of that was in my power?
- What could I have done differently?
- What valuable information have I learnt about myself or my situation?
- What will I try next time instead?

CHALLENGE

Go Out Collecting Nos

If you want a brilliant way to take the sting out of 'failure', make it your mission to go out and collect two 'nos' a week. Taking away the pressure to have everyone say yes is amazingly liberating. Actively seeking to have people tell you 'no' will make you braver and bolder.

And the funny thing is, you'll find it much harder than you think to get the basket load of 'nos' you're after.

Not Knowing is Not a Reason to Stop

A client recently told me her career change journey was making her feel strangely 'untethered'. I thought that was a brilliant description.

Prepare to feel untethered. It's that sensation of drifting, of being unattached, of not yet belonging, that can kill a career change dead before it has really got started.

After all, your identity is in flux. Whilst you feel desperate for something new, not knowing exactly what that looks like can be horribly unsettling because you so badly want to understand who you are and what you want to do. And that can be so uncomfortable at times that you think you should stop.

I warned you about liminal spaces back in Chapter 2, but you've come a long way since then. So here's a timely reminder that being between worlds feels odd. You are on the threshold of something new but not there yet.

Maybe you're getting fed up with people asking what you are doing and not yet having a perfect answer. Perhaps you are carrying the weight of family expectation and it's getting heavy. Or you're frustrated that you can't fully jump from your old life until you have a better sense of the landing you should expect.

Why am I telling you this? Not because there is a magical answer. Change is uncomfortable. I'm telling you because I want you to understand that what you are feeling is not weird, or wrong, or a sign that you should stop. But if nobody tells you that, you can think you are making a hash of it.

Assuming you are committing to taking action to actively engage with your Future Me, you're not making a hash of it.

You're just in the muddle in the middle. Keep going.

The Power of Remembering Your Why

You didn't pick up this book because you wanted a different job. Well, you did, but it was never about simply switching the name of one job for any old other one. The ultimate aim of this process isn't as simple as putting a tick next to the goal marked 'New Career'. It's about what that work represents for you. I asked you three questions at the start of this book:

- What is really important to you about making a change to your work life?
- What difference will a career redesign make to your life as a whole?
- What will it give you that you don't have now?

Your answer may have been monumental or modest. That doesn't matter in the slightest, as long as it was authentic and meaningful. We shouldn't expect our work to give us the answer to everything in life, but as a place where we spend a hefty chunk of time, we each want to choose work that works for us.

When you get bogged down and family life or tiredness get in the way, your Why can start to fade.

It's time to dig out the paragraph you wrote when you started on this journey.

It's the rocket fuel you need to power you forwards.

Chapter 12

Reflections from Career Changers

In the course of writing this book I have spoken to many would-be career changers and people who have already taken the plunge. Some have been my clients, others are people who were happy to share their experiences after travelling the path alone.

For some, their journey has been a long one, shaped by a period of transition while they changed their working pattern, retrained or built a business.

Others have dived in and moved faster, rebranding themselves and heading off into a new sector or industry.

Some people have taken a formal route, involving CVs and interviews and making their case to a new employer. Others have ploughed their own furrow, finding work through their connections, or they've decided to go it alone into the world of self-employment.

Their shift may have involved gaining new skills and a formal qualification, for which they have paid anything from tens or a few hundred pounds for online courses to several thousand pounds for a diploma or degree. They may have self-funded that, been helped by a parent or relative, or found government or grant funding.

For others, the process of refashioning their existing skills into a new form was sufficient to enable them to make their move with no extra study or investment, and in a significant number of cases additional training was given on the job.

The catalysts for the career changers I spoke to were broad, from a desire for money and recognition, to a need for a more flexible work–life balance, greater fulfilment or impact. Most changes were driven by a desire for a new chapter and a fresh career adventure, a few by a sense of necessity after illness, redundancy or a career break.

Each of these people, whether in their twenties, thirties, forties or fifties, came at the process with their own set of assumptions, limiting beliefs, concerns and motivations. Each has had to get to grips with their wobbles, channel and focus their thoughts and self-knowledge, put in the time and do the work.

You have already heard from some of these people throughout the book to illustrate the steps that I am confident will move you forwards towards your own change. But in this last section, I want to give them space to speak at greater length and share more of their personal stories, insights and advice with you. Whilst there are often similarities, everyone's career change story is in some way unique to them.

Dip into these at your leisure and take from them what you need. Their stories are not intended as 'model' cases for you to follow. I have already given you what I believe is the most powerful and practical approach.

These are authentic reflections from a genuine mix of career changers, and I would simply invite you to see what resonates, what you agree or indeed disagree with, what you would do the same or differently, and what that has to tell you about your own journey.

Notice what you notice. That's the point. This is your journey and, armed with my guidance and the experiences of others, you are ready to set off.

EMILY, forties
Public Relations to School Admissions Officer

'I was very nervous. It was nerve-racking. Not having worked for two years, with my maternity leave and then the redundancy, I hadn't put on a dress or makeup in all that time. So it was a big change to all of our lives, and it took some getting used to. But I've relaxed into it.'

Emily spent nine years as the PR manager for a four-site London restaurant chain. She was on maternity leave, with a small baby and a toddler, when the pandemic hit and she was made redundant. Whilst she had always envisaged a change for herself when she hit 40, she had assumed it would be a move within the PR sector. But with the hospitality industry under pressure, she felt herself drawn to the education sector. Her story has plenty of insight about spotting the threads in your career and reshaping your career story for CV and interview. Emily's move also offers a reminder that securing a job isn't the end of your career change and that liminal feeling! She offers her advice on stepping into a new role as a beginner, now that she is six months into her role as head of admissions at a girl's school.

'I was made redundant during Covid and it was incredibly life-changing. I've never not worked. I've never not had my own income. As much as I admire them, I knew I didn't want to be a stay-at-home mum. So it was a big shock to me and it was a massive loss of confidence.

'From a practical, work environment point of view, I realized working locally would be useful because of our kids and because of the pandemic travel issues. I've got a two-and-a-half-year-old and four-year-old, so not working full-time was also going to be preferable.'

Alongside her ideal working environment, the main question for Emily was really asking herself about what she liked to do and how she could put her skills to good use.

'Education and admissions kept coming up. I have a very close friend who's a deputy headteacher and she said she thought that I should become a teacher. I knew I didn't want to be a teacher but I think that sowed a seed in me. I took this friend out for dinner and asked a million questions. There was a lot going on in education, for example with the 'Everyone's Invited' campaign, and other bits and pieces. So I read round a lot and made sure I was informed. My big piece of advice would be to speak to people in your new space, you've got to speak to people.'

Emily applied for several jobs in education and got an interview at a university as a Student Experience Administrator.

'I didn't get that particular job but I found myself drawn to those job descriptions around admissions – the ideas of welcoming and looking after people. I could see a link with my previous PR work for restaurants. Although I never worked as a waitress, the brand, the identity, the warmth was something that I developed. I think the best way of describing it is the "looking after" aspect is what I enjoy doing.'

Emily went on to make a lot of applications but puts her success in landing her current role in school admissions down to the opportunity to write a personal statement.

'I wrote an A4 side, explaining what I'd done and really scrutinizing the job description, pulling out the things that I could find examples of that I've done. I went over the job description many times. I used the personal statement to really develop a narrative about myself and find similarities in the roles. Yes, there were lots of differences in the jobs, but I think finding the themes and nuggets to draw on would be my advice.

'And when I got the interview, they didn't say, "Oh, this is a complete life change, what are you doing?" I was very transparent about my redundancy and so they knew the situation and that I wasn't going back into hospitality. So that didn't come up as an issue – they really gave me a chance. At the interview I had to do an in-tray test. And I was very honest. I said I don't know how to do a mail merge, I've never needed to do a mail merge in my life. So I was quite clear about the skills I did and didn't have and I think they just thought they'd train me. So I guess them being quite flexible about the person was very, very helpful to me. I didn't have any experience and I couldn't lie about it. They were very open-minded. It didn't really come up that it was a completely different role for me.'

As she has settled into the role and delved deeper into it, Emily can see what they picked up on at interview.

'The hospitality side of things is there, because you are looking after people who are applying for their daughters. I am the first face that they see with admissions. I am the first port of call. The first face of the school "brand". The first conversation they have is with me. So there are skills

I've definitely drawn on from my PR role. But there are things that are just completely new. There's a specific schools computer system called SIMS which I've had to learn. I was surprised because in the job description it said that was essential. And I just said no, I've never done that, but they took a chance on me and it's really worked. They've given me quite a lot of training.'

How does Emily feel now she's six months in?

'When I started my new role I was very nervous. It was nerve-racking. Not having worked for two years, with my maternity leave and then the redundancy, I hadn't put on a dress or make-up in all that time. So it was a big change to all of our lives, and it took some getting used to. But I've relaxed into it.

'My advice when you start is just take it slowly. I quickly identified the people in the building who would be great to have on my side and I've drawn on them lots. I think asking to shadow people is very good. So I asked to sit with someone who I thought would be useful and that was really helpful. I think you will get things wrong because it's a new world. And there's a different culture to working in a school, it's a very different proposition. But I think my biggest piece of advice would just be to not worry about making mistakes. And secondly, don't be afraid to ask questions. I think it makes you sound interested, involved, wanting to do the right thing and do a good job, rather than just getting things wrong and worrying in silence. What you can do as a career changer is bring some new ideas, find the opportunities to identify gaps where you can make useful improvements

and recommendations. That's what makes you different
from someone who's done it for 25 years. I've just had a
lovely six-month review. People now all assume I've worked
in schools before, which is a compliment really. Because it
means I fit in. It's a really lovely job.'

KATHERINE, fifties
Traditional Marketer to Web Designer

'I wish I had moved faster. If you are thinking about
changing, don't faff around, because all of a sudden you're
another year older. I knew I wasn't happy but I just didn't do
anything about it. I would definitely say that if you're stuck,
the only way to get unstuck is to take action.'

Katherine's story is quite common among some of the
women I work with. She has a robust career history, can boast
an MBA and an international background in digital marketing.
But her corporate marketing career was put on hold when she
had her family and a seven-year career break followed. In her late
thirties she detoured her skills into running her own stationery
business for a few years, but by her early fifties was wondering
if it was time to return to the corporate world or try something
different. She reflects on how her next step pulled together skills
from many parts of her working life and offers her advice on
going it alone.

'My kids were older, my father, who was my responsibility, had passed away. So I thought, maybe it's time to get back
into the corporate world. But two things happened. First,
I realized that when you're in your fifties it's not that easy

to get back in – especially when your CV no longer screams "corporate"and all your big-name corporate experience happened twenty years ago. And second, Covid hit.'

Finding herself stuck, Katherine took Curious Conversations to an amazing level. Never mind the Ten Thank You Card Challenge (see Chapter 9). She set out to talk to fifty people in their fifties who had made a shift. She called it the 50:50 Project.

'That was really helpful. I just started asking to interview people and to my surprise everyone said yes, so that really boosted my confidence.'

Keen to share the wisdom she discovered more widely, she took the project online via a WordPress website. In doing so, she stumbled upon her next move.

'One day my website got hacked and started sending people to a Viagra site! My husband, who's more of a techie, spent hours on the phone trying to sort it out without any joy. In the end, we decided to start again and move it to Squarespace. I'd done all the creative stuff, but I needed my husband to build the site – or so I thought. But he never had any time and so I thought, screw it – I'll do it. And when I started, I realized not only could I do it, but I was good at it and it's fun. Squarespace is a really good platform and I knew if I was a small business owner, I would love it because it's so intuitive and easy to use. And that was my "Aha!" moment.'

Katherine soon saw that web design for businesses brought together all of her strengths and skills. Her career threads were emerging.

'I realized that my business experience, particularly the time running my own business, could be a big advantage because I'd been in the shoes of others trying to grow a business. Second, all my marketing work had been about how to attract and retain and build loyalty among customers. So I had the customer bit. And then the third bit is the design, which is something that's always been a part of me – from my love of stationery to life drawing as a hobby. And I realized that over the last ten years I'd been learning Photoshop and InDesign and I would need that. I figured I could teach myself some coding and I could learn everything else online. It seemed like the perfect package. And I saw there was a gap in the market for people like me that came to web design through business management rather than graphic design. My conversations had shown me there were a lot of people who start businesses in their forties and fifties. And I thought maybe they'd be happy to work with somebody older, like me, who perhaps takes a different approach – I thought, well, this could be my thing.'

Katherine was getting into action. Mostly self-taught, she improved her skills by taking some online courses and started to find clients close to home.

'I did a bunch of friends' websites and that gave me a small portfolio. I didn't do the sites for free but I did do them at a reduced rate. Plus I did a website pro bono for a local children's charity.'

Whilst moving forwards at a practical level, Katherine was also making the mindset shifts that many career changers wrestle with.

'The challenge is to quiet the negative voice in your head. For example, when I tell people I am a web designer, the voice in my head asks "Are you really, if you didn't go to art school?" I have to remind myself that I know this – I may not have gone to design school, but I have studied it my whole life; I worked side by side with designers and creative directors; I am someone friends and family turn to for creative advice. I also remind myself it's not bad to be a beginner and that the idea of being a beginner is actually exciting. As a beginner your eyes are wide open; you're constantly learning and exploring new possibilities and not doing things on autopilot. And I think this can make it exciting for clients to work with you too because you're going to work harder and push yourself further to prove yourself and make them happy.'

Like all the career changers I've worked with, Katherine has Commitment and Courage in evidence in her journey too. They can be strong traits in people who decide to set up their own business.

'One of the challenges of going it alone is trying to keep up the enthusiasm. Because it can feel hard, right? It's not like you can just say, OK, I'm a web designer now and everybody starts banging down your door to work with you. It's one thing making the decision for yourself personally, but then you need to tell the world, OK this is what we're doing! So it's important to accept that it's going to take some time and there are things you have to do, whether it's social media, building your network, setting goals – whatever is the right thing for your business.'

Katherine makes the point that Industry Immersion continues even once you've started your shift. It's an ideal way to build momentum, support, knowledge and confidence.

'It's great that your friends and family are encouraging, but then you also need another group of people – a professional network that helps and supports you. Other people from related industries, mentors, professional people who you can turn to for advice and maybe even collaborate with. You need to go out and build and nurture that network. In my case, I joined a women's network, connected with people on Facebook and LinkedIn and started going to free online and in-person industry events.

'Don't be afraid to ask people for help even if they are complete strangers. My experience is that if it is a genuine ask and you're nice about it and you're respectful of people's time, they will often say yes. And if they say no, don't worry – someone else will say yes. I've reached out to people in the US – Squarespace and web designers whose work I've seen and admired – and said, "I'm interested in your journey, I'm trying to do the same thing, what do you think?" and they've been really nice and friendly. There are lots of web design Facebook groups where you can seek advice or ask for guidance – say, I'm struggling with this, or I have a client problem, or I don't know how to code this. If you're not wasting their time, then people are helpful. I think it's good karma. It will come back!

'My second reflection is that I wish I had moved faster. If you are thinking about changing, don't faff around, because all of a sudden you're another year older. I knew I wasn't happy but I just didn't do anything about it. I would definitely say that if you're stuck, the only way to get unstuck is to take action. Push yourself harder. I'm afraid to admit that when I start doing things, I don't always think big enough or set myself a bigger challenge even though I am ready for something more.

When there's nobody pushing you, I think that's a real issue. You need to make yourself accountable or find someone to hold you accountable. I know if I promise someone something, I always deliver . . . but I don't always deliver for myself.'

Find out more about Katherine's research project and her web design business:

https://www.the50fiftyproject.com/
https://www.ascendercreative.com/

DAVE, thirties
Travel Industry to Software Developer

'Financially this was always going to be a bit scary, but we were confident that this was just a stepping stone and that ultimately, in a couple of years' time, we would be fine again and hopefully in a better position. We did the maths and decided to take a hit because you live your job so much and it really was affecting my mood at home.'

Dave decided it was time for a rethink when he realized that a fun, bilingual role in the travel industry he'd taken straight out of university had morphed into a job that was no longer recognizable. What started in his twenties as an exciting way to use his French was now, after several promotions, a miserable management role, involving little use of his languages and meant time away from his wife and young family. Dave's story is a typical example of how climbing the career ladder can inadvertently lead us into roles that were never what we had in mind. But how unhappy do we have to be to make a jump? Dave offers his reflections on tightening the family finances to fund a change, why people took a chance on him and the importance of the support he got from his wife.

'I only went to university because everyone else was going. I had no idea what I wanted to do. I was good at languages, so I thought, well, I'll go and do French and Spanish, but to be honest, I went to that university because my best mate was going there. I ended up with a first-class degree but when I was looking for jobs, all I knew was that I wanted to use my French. I just went on to the university jobs portal and found a role called a hotel contractor. They wanted fluent French and I thought, well, that sounds quite good – you get to go and stay in some hotels. I had no interest in tourism, really. I liked travelling but I'm not passionate about hotels or anything like that! I just wanted to use my French. So I went for an interview and got the job.'

The job procuring space in Paris hotels and selling it to online sites was great for a while.

'Then the kids came along and it became a bit much. I was away one week every month so it was hard. And it wasn't badly paid, but it wasn't fantastic. It's one of those jobs where you really have to climb the ladder to get remunerated properly. So I found that I was grabbing every promotion and it didn't matter which area it was. I ended up working with hotels in London, so the whole French aspect was totally gone. I took stock – I didn't really have a passion for travel, I was no longer speaking French and I'd ended up as a manager but I didn't like managing teams. It had become very dry.

'I had a few depressing evenings with my wife, who was putting up with me and my grumpy moods. I would come in from work thinking, my life is terrible, what the hell am I doing? I was just so bored with it.'

Dave was wrestling with a classic career changer's conundrum, real or imagined.

'I felt stuck between two stools, thinking either I go for something I'm passionate about and interested in or I go for something where I can just earn a lot of money. So I looked into things like finance, the stock market, where I figured the hours would be horrible but at least I'd be bringing back a load of money. And it was my wife who pointed out I was being stupid. She said, "I've had enough of you being miserable. You won't enjoy it, stuck in some stockbroker's office in London coming back in the middle of the night with a big pay packet but not seeing the kids." And she was definitely right. She has been a huge, huge driving force in the whole thing. I don't think I would have changed had she not supported me like that because it affects both of us equally, obviously.'

So Dave turned instead to his genuine passion.

'I really had an interest in technology and programming. I'd done a couple of courses, just in my spare time. And I thought well, let's actually take it a bit more seriously. So I bought a 4-month course online for £12.99 from Udemy. And I would come home every evening from work, put the kids to bed at seven, eight o'clock. And then I would just take my laptop and go and sit in the spare room and study for hours. I was also doing it on my commute – as soon as I got on the train my laptop was out. So it was really intense. But I was so determined this time. I had tried doing a few courses before but it was all very leisurely. This time was different, it was my way out. I had, like, a slightly early midlife crisis.

'And although it was hard, I did genuinely really enjoy the studying. I'd actually get excited signing off work thinking, yes, I'm going to get on my computer and do that course. I was enjoying it so much and it went through my head, wow, if I could do this as my job that would be fantastic. I tried and tested it by doing those courses and I did it over a long enough time and didn't get bored of it to be sure it was sustainable.'

Dave's course of study may have been cheap, but he and his wife, an accountant, were aware that starting a job as a programmer was likely to require a pay cut, at least in the short term. The first role he took paid around half his previous salary.

'We didn't have any savings, never had any kind of inheritance money or anything, and we've worked for everything we have. We do have quite a big mortgage and a nice house, which we obviously bought based on our earnings. So this career change period was always going to be a bit scary, but we just cut back on everything that wasn't necessary, and there was quite a lot when we looked at it. I think I was paying over £200 a month for my gym membership, which went straightaway, and things like TV subscriptions. We cut things back for myself and my wife but not the kids, they weren't impacted. And we were confident that this was just a stepping stone and that ultimately, in a couple of years' time, we would be fine again and hopefully in a better position. We did the maths and decided to take a hit, because you live your job so much and it really was affecting my mood at home. And we've managed to make it work.'

Two years on from the initial switch, Dave is in a programming role for a food delivery app and earning more than he was in travel. But how easy was it to initially land work as a career changer in new industry?

'My wife encouraged me to send out some CVs but I was a little bit low on confidence. But she kept posting me links – What about this one? What about this one? I remodelled my CV by putting myself in a programmer's head. I was very waffly in my old CV with big paragraphs of flowery language. And I thought no, they probably just want facts so I made it very concise and clear and presented it in a professional way, making sure I showed how much I knew about technology and tried to lean on my education. I've got very strong GCSEs, A levels, a first-class degree from a good university. So I hoped they would see that they'd be getting someone who learns very well, who picks things up.

'I sent a CV out to a local firm who were looking for a junior iOS developer. They came back to me quite quickly and offered me an interview. I was worried they might laugh at me. When they asked about my experience I'd have to say, "Well, you know, I sort of sat in bed doing a course really." But the in-house recruiter said they really wanted to see me. What I didn't factor in was the emphasis they put on passion. I think they were very impressed with the fact that I'd done the course whilst working full-time in London. They seemed to think that was more important than actually having the skills. Their attitude was we can teach you the skills and send you on courses, we can

see you're committed and that this is a massive passion for
you.

'A lot of the programmers straight out of university just
fall into roles and don't have the motivation I had shown,
and they don't necessarily have the business experience I
had, and I think that's what the firm really appreciated.
Although I was a junior programmer, they never really saw
me as a junior because I had a lot of business knowledge and
they liked that I was more mature. It felt weird being at that
level because I had got quite high up in my previous role,
managing teams and things, but I viewed that first role as an
opportunity because I think you need to get your foot in the
door and from there you can grow.

'Now I feel really fluent in programming, in the same
way I loved my French. I wanted to work in a job where every day
I'm progressing and I'm learning something new, and programming is its own kind of language. Now I write code almost like
I'm writing a letter in French – it just comes out and it works! I
wanted a job where I felt like I was developing myself every day.'

And that difficult decision between an interesting job and a
job that pays well?

'I think I've found a bit of a halfway house, because this is
actually well paid. And what I really like about this industry is
I don't think I will have to necessarily climb the ladder to see a
progression in salary, which is really important to me because
I hated managing. Here you earn more money by being more
experienced. And still doing the things you love.'

CLARE, fifties
Teacher to Digital Marketer

'It was definitely significant that I got that work through someone I know. I realized I had actually met this lady before, so I was a slightly familiar face, and she's lovely, but the main thing was that she was prepared to take a chance on me.'

Clare could perhaps be described as a double career changer. She worked in marketing in her twenties and, once she'd started a family, decided the corporate world was no longer a good fit. When her children were at primary school, she retrained as a teacher, but the experience was not a happy one and rather than join a school full-time she found satisfaction working as a personal tutor and teaching language classes in a school one day a week. Sixteen years after leaving marketing, she decided to return, making her both a career changer and a career returner. Her story offers a cracking example of the power of your own Circle of Connections, as well as demonstrating the 'foot in the door' method of transition.

'Two things happened. The school where I was teaching one day a week had its funding cut and my eldest was at the stage where he was thinking about going to university. And I thought, tutoring isn't going to pay for the university costs, maybe it's time to head back to marketing. But marketing is a very different game these days. The basics stay the same but digital marketing and social media didn't even exist last time I was there! It made me feel so old, how technology has changed.'

Clare was particularly worried about how her career story looked on paper as she set out to change back to marketing.

'It was a nightmare, because you have to put teacher on there but my CV felt like it was in two halves, like – what do they call it – a cut-and-shut car? So I've got the marketing half on one side, a long time ago, and then the teaching, and then the tutoring.'

She knew she had to be ready to explain why teaching hadn't worked out.

'I just had to be honest. Not so honest that I say teaching was just a nightmare, but just that the work–life balance wasn't there.'

Clare's quirky CV made things a little tricky when she started trying to make the change.

'Initially the agencies were all about the education side. They'd send me for an interview for a personnel job in a school because I have a school background – I didn't want to do personnel! But the problem with marketing was that I didn't have the up-to-date experience.'

Her saving grace came from a conversation. Remember my obsession with the power of other people?

'I have a very good friend who I like to go and have a cuppa with and we'd been chatting about my plans and I'd told her I was exploring going back into marketing. Then, weirdly, she just bumped into a friend of hers in the doctor's surgery of all places. The friend was going through cancer treatment and needed someone to start in the marketing department at her company in a couple of days' time and provide six months cover on a fixed-term contract. And our mutual friend said, "Well, I know somebody who wants to go back into marketing!"

'It was definitely significant that I got that work through someone I know. I realized I had actually met this lady before, so I was a slightly familiar face, and she's lovely, but the main thing was that she was prepared to take a chance on me. And when she came back after her treatment, she even asked me to stay on. She said, "What am I gonna do without my Clare?" Everyone needs a Clare, was how she put it!'

It was six months that weren't totally perfect professionally but that powered Clare's transition.

'It wasn't the best job in the world, they were a bit disorganized but it got me back in the game. The lady that I was working with and reporting to was just ever so slightly older than me, so we hit it off straightaway and she just taught me everything. It meant I had something recent on my CV, and while I was there I undertook a CRM (Customer Relationship Management) project. Even having those three little letters on your CV means you've ticked another box in an algorithm. They didn't do a lot of modern marketing there, but it got me a foot in the door to the next thing – everything's a stepping stone. And it was important, because after those six months I went to agencies and was able to say yes, I've done this and I've done that. And I think that's another way of doing it – just being willing to start something and progress from there.'

Clare successfully moved on to a new role, where the German she had used as a teacher was a big plus and she suspects sealed the deal with the European firm.

She is now a big advocate of transferable skills and finds it easy to spot those that link teaching and marketing.

'A headteacher I once spoke to said, "Your skills are completely transferable. As a teacher you have to *market* concepts to young people. In fact, it's more challenging because they're young people and they don't always understand the concept you're selling!" And at the agency that I was recently doing an interview through for my next marketing job, the recruiter was encouraging me, he was like, "Oh for goodness sake, Clare, you used to stand in front of a group of young people and present to them, it'll be a doddle with the team of people you're presenting to today." And of course, it's not quite a doddle but you can make more errors with adults than with children, because children will eat you alive!

'So a lot of those skills *are* transferable. I think you need to look at soft skills. I mean, yes, you need a few specific skills – for me it's CRM systems and content management systems for websites and things like that. But there are so many soft skills – teamwork, for example, is a classic one. As a teacher and as a marketer you have to have really good team skills, and get on with people, and it's those sort of skills that you can get across in an interview, because at the end of the day, if they feel they can work with you, they kind of turn a blind eye to the things you can't do because you can be taught those, but you can't be taught how to be likable. Another classic is organizational skills. You wouldn't believe the to-do list I had as a teacher, and I have a pretty long to-do list now.

So both jobs require being organized, getting a balance and prioritization of tasks.'

As someone who has what might be termed an 'unsuccessful career change' along her journey, how does Clare feel about her work?

'I'm glad I did the teaching, I don't regret doing it, because I would have always wondered whether I should. I suppose I'm a firm believer that things happen for a reason. And it's not the end. This just sounds cheesy and corny, but another door opens. That's how things are. And actually sometimes it's for a reason. I take a lot of learning from that, that it's OK to "fail" at something, you pick yourself up and you learn from it. I think within the education of young people, we're almost not allowing them to fail. We put bubblewrap around them and expect them to go neatly from this stage of life to that to the next. Things don't always go in a straight line. Careers don't go in a straight line, and by the time you get to my age you realize it's gonna be a bit of a wavy line. I don't think I could have done the same thing for the last 25 years, I'd have been bored rigid.'

MATTHEW, twenties
Wealth Manager to Data Scientist

'Whilst there's some risk and a bit of foresight needed in changing sector, it seemed to me that there's definitely something going on in this field of data science and machine learning and artificial intelligence that makes that a good choice. I was thinking about something that would be good in the long term. I'm always trying to think ahead.'

Matthew is a relatively young career changer who made a shift at 26. Perhaps unsurprisingly for a physics graduate, his approach to the move away from wealth management might be described as an analytical one and his Sector Surfing took a calculated form. Drawing on a genuine interest in technology, he consciously decided to target the emerging sector of AI and data science where he could sense growth opportunities, find a more flexible approach to recruitment and where he felt he could meet his work values around impact, interest and financial reward. Matthew's story includes his reflections on what motivated him to move, how he thought through the direction he should go and how he frontloaded unpaid experience on his CV.

'During my degree, I did a number of internships within the financial and investment world and ended up securing a job for a wealth management firm where I had interned. I was an assistant to the portfolio manager, helping him with managing investments and providing investment research. It was interesting at first to learn different things about finance and help the company grow. But how wealth management works and how the financial markets behave doesn't really change that much over time. And while a family might appreciate the help that you give them, if you're a technology person, like me, then it sometimes felt like I was working in a job that could really be automated. The stuff that I found interesting was how you invest different portions of people's money into different kinds of funds and asset classes. That's interesting in a mathematical way, but a lot of the other part of the job was talking to people about tax and markets and what kind of risk level they're comfortable with and that was never going to be particularly interesting to me.'

Matthew was clear on his work values.

'I wanted something interesting – something where I have to use my mind more than in most jobs – and being around like-minded people is important. People who are thinking about technology and science and keep up with current events, smart people.

'I want something that has some impact on the way the world develops. When I did my degree in physics, there was a small part of me thinking about what it would be like to be a professional physicist – to feel that you had discovered something quite important and have your name in a textbook for all time, that's an impact on the world. It doesn't matter whether or not people see it, but it's important just to know that you have impacted the world in some way. I didn't mind whether it was in an academic book or something practical. So in technology, if you helped make the Citymapper app for example, everyone uses that. And you'd be quite proud of yourself if you've helped it to work well.'

And he was also motivated by financial reward.

'Growing up in London, you know, you see the prices the houses are around here and you think there's no way I can afford to live the life that my parents have, and they've given to me, unless I'm quite well off.'

Matthew's natural first future version of himself was to move into what he describes as a more 'serious' job in the financial sector. But he had concerns that his experience was limited to a small firm and believed the big banks he would ideally target would be looking for 'a typical Oxbridge graduate with an economics degree and more experience in a bigger firm'. A limiting belief? You decide. Either way, he decided it was not the immediate pathway for him and that where he wanted to work would have an altogether different vibe.

'At the same time I was always interested in things related to technology and science. And that always seemed like a growing, very interesting field. And I recognized that I did still have the correct kind of skills, programming and maths, to move into a technology role. I thought to myself, if I'm struggling a little bit to get the most interesting jobs that are lucrative in the financial industry, I should probably aim to just time it right and pick the right sector. And whilst there's some risk and a bit of foresight needed in changing sector, it seemed to me that there's definitely something going on in this field of data science and machine learning and artificial intelligence that makes that a good choice. I was thinking about something that would be good in the long term. I'm always trying to think ahead.'

Matthew spoke to people in the industry and those conversations gave him confidence.

'As it's a relatively new industry, it's less formal in some ways and I think there's also a culture in tech of being more open to hiring people who don't come via a formal, typical entry path or university qualification.

'But I did need to spend time making sure I'd learnt various programming skills, because although I had some from university, they weren't completely relevant. I chose to do an online boot camp, which was five months of intensive work. The financial company I was working for did ask whether I wanted to make some kind of part-time arrangement, but I decided to do it full-time because I was living with my parents and I had some money saved up because of that. And I also thought that, you know, getting back from work and then trying to study something, it's a bit hard to do, so I thought it'd be better if I just focused on a full-time course.'

Matthew put in long hours and then started to apply for work.

'I see horror stories online of people who send out hundreds and hundreds of applications and get very little response, but I just tried to send out a few high-quality applications regularly rather than just churning them out. It was a matter of saying the right things and positioning yourself as a useful hire that has the right kind of experience and has worked on similar things and is not just a fresh graduate who might not have relevant experience.

'I made a one-page CV, because I'm fairly young and that is generally recommended for someone my age without a long work history. My past experience wasn't always particularly relevant, so I just had a small education and experience section and the rest was projects and skills and how those have been of value. I spelled out the relevant experience, talking about projects I'd worked on in my own time, little bits of work for companies that I'd done for free. The course

I'd done recommended you undertake fairly long projects that are similar to what people do in a work environment, and they'd suggested you talk to people in companies and see if you can directly help them in some way with your project. I'd been able to find a video game company that I made something for that they found useful and I'd talked to people in specific financial firms that I was hoping to apply to and I was able to make something for them that they found interesting. I probably did four or five relatively large projects, so I did invest quite a large amount of time in that.'

Matthew is upfront about his 8-month career change journey.

'It was pretty intensive work. I'd just say consider it carefully, maybe take some steps to make sure if the process does take longer, you're OK with that. That might mean working part-time, I could have done that. Maybe in hindsight I should have done that.'

Matthew now works for a company that provides tech services for local councils and the public sector. It's a junior position but he believes he will get where he wants to be.

'Status for me isn't about other people. Because while it might be impressive to say, oh, I'm a data scientist, I do some interesting thing to do with artificial intelligence, most people don't know what that is! So that doesn't really concern me. I think I'm more concerned with how I see myself. Not really status even, but just being seen as an intelligent person. I value that more than status.'

VICTORIA, forties
Publisher to Nurse

'I think this is a hard age for women, perhaps for all of us, actually. We might have parents who are ailing, and teenagers who are moving away from us, we might be peri-menopausal, so I think this is when we probably need to focus on ourselves. I feel changing career has given me a real boost . . . the idea of winding down at forty-seven or forty-eight is just nuts to me.'

Victoria had worked in publishing for 25 years and had recently settled into what she felt was a lovely job, commissioning books for a small publisher with a friendly team. The hours were good and she could walk to work. Then Covid hit and the owner of the company decided to close the business. Victoria's story has practical insights on making your case as a career changer, as well as some interesting reflections on success and shifting careers later in life.

'It was a really difficult moment because we were just coming out of lockdown and I was thinking, what am I going to do now? I realized that I just wanted to work and be stimulated rather than climb a ladder or rise up through a company. I just wanted a busy job where I'd be satisfied. I narrowed it down to opening a book shop or becoming a nurse. I've always been very interested in anything to do with the body. Everyone says I'm the least squeamish person you can find. When I worked in publishing I oversaw lots of health books, particularly on the human body, because I'm a bit obsessed! I've always had a fascination, and I've watched countless TV documentaries on operations. So I guess the idea of nursing had been lying there, unconsciously.'

Victoria signed up for a three-year nursing degree and is excited by the possibilities this opens up, from general nursing in a hospital to becoming a specialist nurse, working at a GP practice or even as a school nurse.

'I'd always felt a bit odd reading medical books, but the first thing I did when I started nurse training was to listen to Bill Bryson's *The Body*, and I loved the fact that I could now legitimately listen to this book without feeling like a weirdo!'

The application hadn't been without its challenges, but it neatly demonstrates the experiences, skills and interests that are pulled together in Victoria's new career path.

'I had to write my personal statement and I thought that meant just a paragraph. Then I started looking them up online and saw that the process was much more involved; I racked my brains about my transferable skills. I wrote about how I'm fascinated by the human body. And how I felt I was a caring person. And I thought broadly – I've run a family and I have two children who I love and look after, and my father had a stroke five years ago and I spent four months going into hospital three or four times a week to help look after him. So I'd had direct experience of what it is to help people. And I'm someone who just gets on with stuff. You know what I mean? And actually, to be a nurse, you just need to get on with stuff.

'At the interview they asked me why I wanted to become a nurse and I just said, "I love people, I'm fascinated by the human body and I'm caring." I think that's really all I could say at that point. And I knew that I worked hard. I knew that a shift didn't scare me, being in hospital didn't scare me. And interestingly, there are aspects of nursing that a lot of trainee nurses are not prepared to do and it's been commented on on the ward, the fact that I really don't mind doing anything – I don't know if that's because I'm a bit older. If I have to sweep a floor, I'll just go and do it, as long as I get to do something interesting like putting in a catheter or taking blood as well. You find yourself brushing people's hair, cleaning people's teeth, alongside taking blood, trying to analyse blood test results, figuring out what's wrong with someone. It's both. I love looking after someone holistically. It's very special and fulfilling.'

Victoria is upfront about the finances and logistics.

'I've got student loans to pay for the teaching, which I will have to pay back when I am earning a certain amount; I'm not really terribly worried about it right now. My husband has a good salary, a normal salary, nothing crazy. In my case, from a practical point of view, I have twins who are doing their GCSEs this academic year, so they are working hard and becoming more independent. This is a good time for me to focus on my career and place more demands on my life like working long shifts.'

In her case, the move from freelance work to employment has also been significant.

'A couple of years ago I was so daunted by the next twenty years, thinking, am I going to be freelance all my life? Now having experienced working life in a hospital, I can't compare this to my previous working life. It's exciting in the hospital. I get to work with all kinds of talented and highly skilled people instead of being on my own editing books . . . I thought I suited freelancing and I was very nervous about going into the hospital because I thought I was better working on my own, but working with these other lovely nurses, who support you, has given me more confidence.

'I'm fascinated by the workings of the hospital and why people are in there. You're in a place where life and death happens. I'm in a place where major operations are being done, highly skilled people are working, and that is very exciting to me. You have to work where you're interested. Otherwise, you're not going to fully engage with it.'

What reaction has she received to her midlife shift?

'A few people strangely have said, "Wow, what a thing to do. You know, at your age. Some people are already really winding down at this point." But the idea of winding down at forty-seven or forty-eight is just nuts to me. I think this is a hard age for women, perhaps for all of us, actually. We might have parents who are ailing, and teenagers who are moving away from us, we might be peri-menopausal, so I think this is when we probably need to focus on ourselves, because it's a hard time. I feel changing career has given me a real boost. I hope I've fended off the middle-aged depression a bit!

'I know that it is common to struggle at this stage of life, and I would have done had I not taken on this change. Two years ago, I was asking, "What am I going to do?" It's really hard and I think your confidence can be a little lower than it should be, because although we have loads to offer, we have so much experience, for some reason workplaces are so attuned to younger faces, and that's very difficult, isn't it?

'I have no regrets, like not even a tiny bit. The only thing I'm scared about is the responsibility and the weight that goes with having to look after people, administering medications and knowing what's wrong with people, but that's not a bad thing. It can be daunting. If it goes well, I'm sorted for the next twenty-five years! I feel like for the first time in my life I know what self-actualization is. I've never felt more enriched. It's taken a long time to get there, and I know it's going to be difficult and stressful, but I'm really proud of what I have done.'

ANTHEA, fifties
Project Manager to Funeral Director

'You can't quite believe every day some of the things that happen and what you deal with and what you see. It's like an obsession. You just can't believe you're doing this job. I didn't ever expect to be out with a top hat on conducting or leading a service.'

After a somewhat mixed career journey, Anthea hit midlife looking to re-evaluate her work life and find a truly satisfying way to pull together her skills. She had started her career working for a travel company, then taken a career break to raise a family, during which time she worked part-time as a massage therapist. Her own house renovation then led to ten years in the construction industry as a project manager for the builder who had done the work. When his business hit problems, she set up on her own but knew it wasn't quite right. Anthea's story is a fantastic example of finding work that draws on different parts of your career to date and a testament to the powerful and surprising results of taking real action to explore your ideas!

'I was working with individuals who needed building advice, a little bit of interior design, helping them choose things, coordinating tradesmen, overseeing payments, and it was fine. I was good at it but I wasn't really enjoying doing the work on my own. I just knew I didn't feel 100 per cent. It was a bit of a chore. I wasn't very good at charging for myself and work was completely all-consuming. It felt quite lonely because you're not with a team any more and you're not part of anything.

'I think I knew I was ready to do something different because my kids were growing up. I wanted to get into something properly. I didn't particularly want to go work in an office and just do more admin for somebody else. And I did think about whether to retrain completely in something new, but I didn't really want to do a ton more exams, because I found that really challenging.'

So Anthea started tuning in to what she enjoyed and what she was good at and how it was already showing up in small ways in her life. The question 'What do people turn to you for help with?' might have been made for her! (Check out 'The Other Yous' exercise in Chapter 3.)

'Around the same time, a family friend died who I'd been helping over several years with admin and PA type work, just on the side from my day job. She had in place quite specific instructions for her funeral, so I helped her husband coordinate everything. She lived locally to me but she wanted a green burial near Brighton and the funeral director who came to the house to discuss it was a woman and it really struck me that she was just the nicest, most sensible, organized, calm, person. Not what I expected at all. She was brilliant. So we organized the funeral, which, after all, was really just another project management thing but on a personal level. I organized a memorial service in London as well, the service and the flowers and the catering afterwards. Once I'd overseen that one funeral, people heard about it and sought out my advice for their own family. People would say, you should ask Anthea! And the whole funeral thing just kept tapping me on the shoulder. And at the same time, a friend who had previously given me advice on my career and gently tried to push me out of my comfort zone said, "Why don't you do that yourself?"'

It was time for Anthea to see if she was on to something with her idea and test if it really was a possible Future Me.

'I literally googled the nearest funeral directors to my house, called them and offered my time for free because I knew nothing about funerals or dead bodies or anything. The woman I spoke to said, "Yes, we always need a bit of help. You're welcome to come in."'

A half-term holiday followed and by the time Anthea was due to go in the woman she had made the arrangement with had left her job, it later transpired to set up in business on her own.

'She wasn't around when I called to confirm my visit, but the funeral director told me to come in anyway. He asked if I'd ever seen a dead body before and I said only my granny when I was ten. He showed me a lady in the Chapel of Rest. It was a bit of a test. And I was fine about it. I really was quite surprised at myself. He showed me around then, and it's a small independent funeral directors, doing everything from collecting to the funeral and beyond, gravestones and everything. And he said, "Would you like to come in tomorrow and spend the day? Because it's a funny job and it's not really for everybody." And I came on that Thursday and I never left!'

The sudden departure of the member of staff meant they were recruiting. Anthea was a great fit.

'Very rapidly I was doing a 60-hour week, which I still kind of do. I love it. I absolutely love it. And every day it's challenging in more ways than you can think. But it's really good. I never would have thought, oh, I want to be a funeral director. I probably wouldn't even have thought it was a job that I would be able to do. I don't even particularly know how I would have trained for it. You can go the whole qualifications route but I just dived in the deep end and there we are.'

When I ask Anthea for the threads that are pulled together in her new role, she is quick to see them.

'It's great. It uses all my skills from my work to date, even the work I used to do as a massage therapist for a time, when my children were small. So every little bit along the path of my career to date is somehow represented. The practical side is all the administration and finances, which uses the organized bit of my brain and my project management background. But the bit I really like is the human side. Which is the bit that came from my work as a massage therapist – where clients become friends, and people – yes, they wanted a massage, but often they really wanted to offload or talk. So I enjoy giving good advice and almost being a phone-a-friend for people at a really tough time. I've always been a community-minded person. It's great all the different people who walk through our door. We do all kinds of funeral – non-religious, Sikh, Hindu, Muslim, Catholic, Afro-Caribbean and they are all different. Meeting these families and understanding different cultures is fascinating. And I'm a creative person – not arty or anything, but there are really nice creative things that you can do to make a funeral really personal and meaningful. And it doesn't need to cost loads of money. It's not all about the shiny car, horse and carriage and all of that.

'So when people say to me, you know, I'm looking for a job and, to be honest, I just want to work and come home and not worry about it . . . well, that's definitely not this job. I mean, I worry about it 24/7, you know! The things that I personally feel are the bits I get most value out of are the creative extra bits and all of that kind of thing.

'You know it's a good fit because you do it well and you enjoy coming to work. I've ended up in a position where I have a lot of power, I suppose. Not that I really call it that, but I have a lot of influence in the way the business runs and what decisions we make and all of that kind of thing. And it's really nice. It's a proper career and I just never expected to have a proper career. The fact that there was a place around the corner that I can walk to from home, the fact that this woman had chosen to leave . . . the stars aligned!

'People say to me it's so completely right that you're doing this, my friends know how happy I am. And it's been a really, really, really good fit for me. You can't quite believe every day some of the things that happen and what you deal with and what you see. It's like an obsession. You just can't believe you're doing this job. I didn't ever expect to be out with a top hat on conducting or leading a service.'

STUART, thirties
Lawyer in a Media Company to
Lawyer for a Philanthropic Foundation

'I was more or less at the stage of giving up on law because I didn't think I could be happy as a lawyer, but it turns out I just needed the right job and to work towards a cause that I care about.'

What kind of career change is lawyer to lawyer, I hear you wonder! It might strike you as strange but Stuart considers it a 'complete career transformation', which he wouldn't have believed possible two years previously. I believe his story is more than worth telling because it is a brilliant example of someone who decided to change rather than to chop, a concept I invited you to consider back in Chapter 5. And for Stuart it had an extraordinary effect. He had been so miserable at work he was on the verge of quitting his job as legal counsel at a media company. But by considering what he wanted to preserve, what he needed to alter and how many pathways within his own industry there were that he had not yet explored, he turned his career around. His story also offers an insight into the way work unhappiness can sap our energy and confidence and how other people can hold the key to the next step.

> 'I took a law degree, although I'm not sure why. It felt like the choice was doctor or lawyer. My dad was a lawyer, but I didn't really have any careers guidance and it turned out I hated the course.'

After university, Stuart worked for a while as a lawyer for a publishing company before making a brief foray into teaching. Partway through his training he realized being a teacher wasn't for him and went back to the law, this time as legal counsel at a media company. But it wasn't long before doubts resurfaced.

Stuart had a strong set of work values – intellectual stimulation, authenticity, loyalty, influence, equality, compassion, curiosity – and had no trouble identifying what elements of his job were and weren't working for him.

> 'I really liked my colleagues and enjoyed the people I worked with. I liked dealing with legal problems and feeling my brain work. But a lot of the day-to-day work was repetitive and uninteresting. It wasn't helping people.

I was working with clients in oil, alcohol and tobacco and felt like no one really cared about stuff that was really important.

'I wanted a career that I found more fulfilling, that I could get passionate about, that I could feel was worthwhile and meaningful. It felt important to me to do something that helps people and is useful to society. I'm willing to work hard, but I need to care about what I'm doing. I much prefer the idea of a vocation to a job.'

A common result of feeling unhappy at work is a corresponding decline in self-confidence. Stuart was no exception.

'I started to actually believe the strengths I needed as a lawyer – reasoning skills, advocacy, processing information and so on – weren't my strengths at all. I had a performance review coming up and I felt so negative about my skills and how I was doing, I really felt I needed to start with an apology to my boss! All the things I felt I wasn't doing well were at the forefront of my mind. I didn't like my job but it was hard to find any motivation to change because I felt lost. I felt trapped.'

That fall in energy can show up in other parts of life when we are unhappy at work.

'I knew what would be good for me – writing, exercise, meditating, seeing friends, doing other things that made me happy – but I lacked the drive to actually do them.'

Finding his Why and painting a powerful picture of his ideal work life helped Stuart gradually refocus.

'In this imaginary new future I would be engaged, happier, an authority, a trusted colleague, invested in my work, producing something worthwhile with a real sense of collective purpose. I would have passion and energy and feel like what I was doing was really helping people.'

Stuart was looking at several future versions of himself. One – a move into writing or journalism – felt like too a big leap for the time being for a young man starting a family and taking on a mortgage. He felt he needed to listen to his head *and* his heart.

'I really disliked my job but now that I'd spent a lot of time and money training to be a lawyer, I knew I would find it difficult to change course, especially because we had a young daughter and were in the process of buying a house. So the question was how could I use my skills and training for something more meaningful? Find a more fulfilling job that pays the bills!'

Stuart identified areas of law he was interested in that were far more aligned with his values: human rights, charity law, environmental law. But he was disheartened by the feeling that he might need an additional qualification.

'Most of the people working for the organizations I had in mind seemed to have a master's degree in environmental law. I looked into postgraduate courses out of interest, but they were expensive and time-consuming, so not an option for me.'

A month before the UK lockdown Stuart handed in his notice at the media company.

'I didn't have another job lined up but I just decided I had to take the leap. It was quite rash really, but shortly afterwards I spoke to a recruiter who put me in touch with the general counsel at an independent philanthropic organization, working with a range of partners seeking to transform the lives of children and young people. Among other things they fund a lot of work around the world tackling climate change, which was something I really wanted to get involved in.'

Stuart got on well during his Curious Conversation with the in-house lawyer. The seed was sown and when someone left the team a couple of months later, he was offered a job as legal counsel. It started as a transition – it was initially on a temporary basis – but became permanent.

'I'm so happy in my new job. They funded me to do a climate change law course and I got to go to COP26 for some meetings and a conference. In a brilliant coincidence, one of the environmental charities I'd often thought I'd love to work for turns out to be one of the charities we fund, so I get to work with the team there on a daily basis!'

Stuart offers some useful reflections on the biggest things that needed to change for him.

'I was more or less at the stage of giving up on law because I didn't think I could be happy as a lawyer, but it turns out I just needed the right job and to work towards a cause that I care about.

'I needed to rethink my options and think more creatively about how I wanted to move forwards, and to look at my thought patterns and habits. It was really powerful for me to think about my core values and how I might craft a career around those values. I needed to understand myself better to better understand the direction I should steer my career to allow me to be happier and more fulfilled.'

SARAH, forties
Veterinary Nurse to Soft Tissue Therapist

'It's the best, best thing that I've ever done because it's my business, my rules. I fit it around family, I don't have to answer to anyone.'

Sarah worked as a veterinary nurse for over twenty years. She took a career break when she had her two daughters and gradually went back to work part-time. It wasn't long before she realized she was ready for a change. Her story is a great example of the how your interests, hobbies, abilities and existing experience can combine to shape your next chapter. She also shares what was hard and what she loves about starting her own business as a soft tissue therapist.

'Veterinary nursing isn't a horrible job, it's a great job. But I just got bored. I stopped learning and I think the moment you stop learning, stop having a passion for what you do, you're not in the right job any more. And it just so happened whilst I was still doing a little bit of part-time vet nursing, my eldest daughter started gymnastics. They knew I'd done gymnastics as a kid so they said come and do some coaching.

I wasn't sure at the time that I wanted to do it, but five years later I was still coaching and had completed qualifications.

'Over time, with the gymnastics coaching, they sometimes had kids getting injuries and I was curious to help. So I researched around that and got really interested. I started learning how to tape up knees, that sort of thing. I got somebody in to provide them with treatments and support.'

Added to that, Sarah was herself extremely active and sporty.

'I've always been quite active, quite sporty myself – running, swimming, Tough Mudder courses and that sort of thing. I'm a lover of mud! And I'm really, really good at injuring myself! So I have a lot of experience myself of seeing therapists, osteopaths, sports massage, you name it. I'd probably always had quite an interest, read a lot around it.

'And I started to think I could do this job – what you're doing, I could do that job. And I've got the bonus of all the animal medical knowledge from my veterinary nursing. So I had an initial chat with the woman who used to treat me every couple of weeks. She suggested a few places and I looked into it, and the reason that I was able to do it was that she told me about a course that was nowhere near as expensive as a university degree. I had also thought I couldn't give up the time because my kids were the age they were, but this course was only thirteen months long. My grand-mother had passed away a year before and I had some money from her sat there. And I was like, you know what, I think she'd be really proud if I used it for this. And I qualified just over five years ago.'

So the elements came together and Sarah now sees more children and adolescents than other therapists in her area because of her experience working with them and being familiar with their conditions and their rehab. She looks back on her journey.

'The course was hard, with children and trying to run a house. It wasn't a full-time course, it was a weekend away every month but a lot of assignments, a lot of clinical hours. So you have to be pretty determined. And our course didn't have any business modules in it at the time, so, you know, you qualify, you've got all this knowledge and you're like, where are the people? I probably made all the mistakes that I could have done with paying a fortune to chuck my name in the Yellow Pages, leaflet drops, all the stuff that I now know is an absolute waste of time. So I've made all the mistakes. Now I'm always happy to share what's worked and what hasn't in therapist Facebook groups. I think you need to realize that, on average, it takes two to three years to build up a reasonable business. It doesn't happen overnight. It's hard work and you have to keep at it.

'But it's the best, best thing that I've ever done because it's my business, my rules. I fit it around family, I don't have to answer to anyone. I'm really passionate about what I do, so I like things done well and I want them done properly, and it really irritates me if they aren't. So I know that what I do, it's done to the best of my ability, and that's what I try and strive for in my business. And every day I'm reading things, learning things, and I'm as busy as I want to be.

'There's such a satisfaction from being good at what you do, from making people feel better. You're not taking people's pain away, but you're educating them how to feel better, how to look after themselves. That was always the driving force. And it's not just people who do sport that I see. You know, I see people with ME, with cancer, a wide range of people. So you can make such a difference in a small way for one person. I also use my skills to volunteer at a hospice with people in palliative, end-of-life care. It's just giving them a nice massage, to make them feel better in that moment. And what's more valuable than that?'

Looking ahead, Sarah has also been asked to teach on the course which she herself took.

'These little extra things keep popping up. So it's morphing into a bigger thing now, which I think is a good challenge. And the tutoring position will give a little longevity if I can't do my job any more for physical reasons, because it is a physical job. That's a backup. So I'm always learning. And the minute that stops I'll know that I'm in the wrong profession, but I don't think it will.'

See more about Sarah's business:
https://www.affinitybodyworks.co.uk/

FIONA, forties
Graphic Designer to Stone Carver

'My thought is to reduce the graphic design to maybe one day a week. I'm on the cusp now of taking the jump. I've done the maths in my head and I think it would be fine. I like to think that one day I will be wholly working on my stone commissions.'

Fiona is a what I'd call a long transitioner. A graphic designer by profession, she has spent a decade honing her craft in stone work alongside her paid job, with a bit of stopping and starting to allow time for two children along the way. What started out as a hobby has become a growing letter-carving business. Now it offers a reliable source of income, she is wondering about the balance of her future career. Her story is an interesting study of how career change can be a slow burn rather than intensive, involving a portfolio of work. It also touches on the way our natural interests can show up long before we formalize them into a career and how noticing what we do and don't enjoy about our current work can help us take our next steps. It's also worth noting how outside funding has played a role in facilitating Fiona's career change and the option of a portfolio career.

> 'I'd always been creative at school. I did a graphic design degree and when I was at university, pretty much all of the work was done by hand, cutting out the type, the page layouts, and we had a small amount of work on a computer, very tiny Macs. And that's what I liked, making with my hands. But then I started to work in a design agency and so much of the work was all computer-based.'

Fiona is easily able to identify the bits of her work she did enjoy – her Starring Roles – and find clues as to why she hasn't been fulfilled.

> 'My favourite type of activity at work was always making the mock-ups, the brochures and books and physical

point-of-sale pieces, actually physically making those. So after many years of sitting at a computer, learning software, I started to get a bit disheartened. I do like the creative side of the graphics, it's just sitting at the computer that I don't particularly enjoy.'

Initially she sought to scratch her maker's itch outside of work, taking evening classes in subjects from pottery to cabinet making. It was tapping into an interest she could chart back to her childhood, just as I invited you to consider back in Chapter 6 (see 7 Ways to Unearth Your Interests).

'Both my dad and grandad were carpenters and as a child I liked hanging around their sheds . . . the smell and trying to make things in there. And I always liked architecture and wanted to be an architect at one point when I was looking at career options at school. I was probably about 14 and I think it was the training that put me off!'

Fiona can point to many instances when the seeds of her stone-carving business were being sown.

'I was saying to someone the other day that the first bit of stone lettering I noticed is when I went to my grandad's funeral and there was a headstone near his that was hand-carved. I didn't know it was, I just knew that it was beautiful. It was very simple but had lovely lettering on it. And I was really taken with it. And that was a long time before I started.

'And I remember a period when I went travelling during my twenties. While I was away, I was always looking at the buildings and surrounding nature – I spent a lot of time in

Australia and saw so much open space, nature, rocks but also architecture. When I was in New York, there were people doing stone carving on a church, cutting the stone in situ. In Singapore, I saw men working on a building, doing a similar thing but in a completely different material, more of a clay, modelling shapes on to a building. And someone I met in a desert in Australia was carving things into talc and rocks. I even came back with a little collection of stones from different places!'

Returning home from her travels, Fiona was watching her local TV news when a story came on about how a generation of stonemasons were dying out because no one was learning the skills. It featured a place that ran courses.

'I thought, well, why wouldn't you want to learn that? So I found them and booked on to pretty much all their courses, did the weekend courses and found that the carving and the lettering was what I really enjoyed.'

For a number of years, Fiona spent holidays and weekends studying and fine-tuning her skills whilst continuing to work as a graphic designer. She applied for scholarships and funding so she could do longer courses. For a time she did an apprenticeship for two days a week. Awards and bursaries that she found out about through artists organizations, specialist newsletters and being part of the broader carving community made quite a difference to Fiona's journey. They allowed her to undertake additional study, learn from experienced craftspeople and buy specialist equipment.

Having met many carvers through her courses, Fiona felt confident that being a letter cutter was a viable and worthwhile career choice and she just needed practice to increase her cutting speed. She got her first commissions – a house sign closely followed by a memorial – through word of mouth.

Through her lettering work, Fiona knows all about the state of flow (see page 68).

'It's not about whacking the stone. Doing lettering is calmer, kind of therapeutic. You get into a particular state and you have to really concentrate. Everyone always asks me what do you do if you make a mistake and I say we don't make mistakes! I don't know how to describe it, but it's like people who do mindfulness. You're there and that's what's happening. And if I try and do a little bit when the kids are upstairs or doing something else, l go in the workshop and I'll still be there three hours later.'

A decade on from her first forays into stone work, Fiona is busy and considering taking her graphic design work down to one day a week.

'Things have really picked up this last year. I think a lot of the letter cutters have all been really busy. I've got stone work that is needing my attention and more jobs to quote on and I don't have enough time. At the moment I split my working hours 50/50. I still enjoy the creative side of graphic design and the portfolio career is mostly working well for me at the moment. I'll be reviewing the balance as my stone commissions increase. My thought is to reduce the graphic design to maybe one day a week. I'm on the cusp now of taking the jump. I've done the maths in my head and I think it would be fine. I would like to think that one day I will wholly be working on my stone commissions.

'I'd say, if you are thinking about or need to change careers, do it. Find something that you enjoy or makes you happy and fulfilled. Your lifestyle may need to change but a career that offers a richer life experience and a better family and work–life balance is worth the effort – even if at times it doesn't feel like it is and the process takes longer than you originally thought!'

You can see Fiona's work at:
http://www.stonecreationstudio.com/

FREDDIE, thirties
Actor to Nurse

'Your story is yours to tell and only tell as much of it as you want to. And if you're not ready to tell it, don't tell it. You can say, "Well, actually, I'm looking at new options now. And I'm in the middle of having a rethink," and I think maybe that kind of language is easier for people to understand.'

It was clear to Freddie from an early age that he would find narrowing down his future self tricky – his story may read like someone who struggled to make up their mind. Actually, Freddie has come to see the common threads in his career decisions very clearly and shares a powerful narrative around what drives him professionally. Although he is clearly inspired and motivated by his move into nursing, he speaks honestly about the frustrations that brought him there and the discomfort and sadness of letting go of a ten-year acting career. I wanted to share his story – not just to highlight the practicalities of his career change but because it raises insightful questions about the constraints and values we put on careers and offers authentic ways to speak about change.

> 'I always begin by saying I applied for courses in English, medicine and drama on the same personal statement. I've never got over that particular foible. But I did it because when I was eighteen, those were the things that really, really drew me and I was indignant, and still am, at the idea that you have to be more focused so early on. English was my favourite subject and I was really good at it, I got full marks and I loved it. Medicine is something that I could always see myself doing, it was always an interest. And then drama. I must have done hundreds of plays in my local theatre, growing up. I've always, always, always wanted to be an actor.'

Perhaps unsurprisingly, the fairly rigid application system rejected Freddie's mixed messaging and he didn't get the place that he wanted at university. He took a gap year and worked in his local hospital in their renal unit as a nursing assistant.

> 'It was hard work, long hours, but I enjoyed it. I enjoyed the patient contact and I enjoyed the human situations.'

Second time around, Freddie landed a place to study education with English and drama, which he loved. Three years later he won a coveted place at drama school and successfully got acting work soon after he finished.

> 'But you do a job and it doesn't necessarily lead to another job. You then go back to square one and you're chasing the next thing, and it was a really difficult time. I remember sitting on some steps in Covent Garden on a

Tuesday morning and thinking, well, everyone else has got somewhere to be, and something to do. And I don't and I'm sitting here no use to anybody. I just hadn't prepared myself psychologically for the idea that there's all this downtime. I'd never had any downtime before, these big yawning gaps. And most people at least had some form of nine-to-five to keep them busy. And then of course you'd take all the temp jobs in between the acting stuff and I didn't find those very fulfilling. Most actors don't, because you're trying to do something reasonably flexible that means you can drop it if acting work comes up.'

Freddie gave the acting world ten years, during which time he also co-founded a small theatre company which provides entertainment for private parties and corporate functions. But as life moved on, and the life of an actor continued to be precarious, he realized it was time for a change, not least because his husband was quick to see how unhappy he was.

'He could tell I was walking around with a big hole in my life. It is like carrying a grief. I had this need, this desire, and I went all guns blazing for an acting career and you commit everything to it and when I was working it was euphoric. It was like a drug. I loved it. And I was good at it. And then I couldn't, I just couldn't get more of it. I couldn't get it in the way that I wanted to.'

It was time to look back and find his work values and his career threads.

'I had a biology teacher at school who gave me the best piece of advice I've ever had which was Freddie, you are interested in the human condition. It sounds really pompous, but I think it's actually one of the kernels of the things that do interest me. It's what interests me about acting. I didn't want to go on stage to get the applause at the end. But I did want to spend eight weeks exploring why these human beings were talking to each other in this way.

'I decided to look back to some of those kernels that really obsessed me as I was going through my higher education journey. Is there more that I can give? Is there more that I can do? Are there ways that I would find more fulfilling to fill up my time on this earth? I realized I derive a lot of my pleasure and my sense of peace from being of use and being of service to other people.'

Freddie's exploration took him back to his gap year in the renal unit and he signed up for a two-year MSc in Nursing.

'I'm aware it's a huge privilege because it can cost a lot to retrain. I don't have children. I have a husband who earns well. So if I wanted to, I could go back to school. And that's what I chose to do.

'I have found that in the 18 months that I've been training, the thing that I respond to is that human condition out there on the table in all its unfathomable, interesting, difficult, joyful, tragic glory. So it's the spirit of that which I've been chasing, I think all my life, trying to navigate a pathway where I wasn't going to be career-focused but human-condition focused and see where that takes me.'

The change has required more than long hours in Covid

wards, palliative care and A&E. It has required the discomfort of 'what do you do?' questions at parties and making peace with a different pathway.

'Your story is yours to tell and only tell as much of it as you want to. And if you're not ready to tell it, don't tell it. You can say, "Well, actually, I'm looking at new options now. And I'm in the middle of having a rethink," and I think maybe that kind of language is easier for people to understand. So when people ask me about leaving acting, I say it's still a love for me and something that I carry with me. I'm not a different person now. And it's not like I don't want to talk about the last ten years, but I'm doing this now because this is going to give me, I hope, a richer future. So it's owning it. And you don't have to explain it to anyone, but you also shouldn't hide it away because it's part of what's pushing you towards something else.

'A career change is a bit like when a relationship ends – I think the worst thing people can say to you is "That's the best thing that could have happened" or "I never liked them anyway" or "You're so much better without them". Because that can invalidate months, years, whatever time, emotional energy and growth that they've put into their relationship or career, it invalidates all of that in a swoop. Every part of your career is part of your history. We can take it with us if we need to, or we can put it down when it serves.

'We do live in a world where a great deal of our validation and self-worth comes from the work that we do and that's because we spend a lot of time doing it. If you can't give a name to what you want to do, you are immediately a slightly alien presence in a room, when most other people can, and that's a difficult space to occupy when you're changing careers. Because, of course, often there's no short answer, and people really are sort of asking for the short answer.

'But more broadly – and I think this is happening – it will be helpful if we can all understand that we're not defined by the job that we do and we're not defined by the career that we have, in the way that we used to be, when you'd go in apprenticed at eighteen and you'd leave with your crystal fruit bowl at seventy. I think we're all understanding that that doesn't happen now. I want to do more, give more, be more with my time.'

KERYS, forties
Journalist to Teacher

'You know when you go to a job interview and they ask why you want the job? I know a good answer isn't "Well, you know, it's really practical. I can't get a job in journalism and I want the school holidays." But for me that was what was behind it. And then you learn to like it after that. You know, as you get good at it. You learn to become passionate about it.'

Kerys is an unusual career changer, who is very honest in saying her move from journalism to teaching was driven by practical motivations rather than desire. A happy and fulfilling career on newspapers became impractical once she and her husband started a family, and her desire for flexible working was met by rejection. A longer-than-planned five-year career break followed, before Kerys set out to find a career that would work for her and allow her to build something new and lasting. Following a stint as a classroom assistant, she is now a successful teacher, a role that she says she has learnt to become passionate about. She is studying for a master's with a focus on special needs teaching and mental health in schools.

Her story is an interesting study in hard choices, transferable skills and the many different things from our career profile that can drive our career choices. I share it because I believe being honest with yourself about what you want and why is an important part of any career change and takes everyone to a different place.

'My husband is also a journalist and actually that's how we met – we had exactly the same job. Same pay, same group of friends, same lifestyle. And then we had kids and that changes everything in a way that I just didn't realize. So, you know, I wanted to come back to work. But now I couldn't do the same hours any more. I couldn't.

'When my eldest went to primary school and my youngest went to kindergarten I needed to get a proper job. I went for so many freelance, part-time journalism jobs and I would get down to the final three, but the fact that you're the one with kids made it tricky. In one interview, they laughed at me. It was like, you know, if you want to work for us, of course everyone's going to have to work nights. And I thought, right, that's it with journalism. I'm going to stop bashing my head against the door, this isn't happening. Which was a shame, because journalism was what I really wanted to do, it was a great job.

'I felt guilty for not having a job really. And also because my husband had to work extra hard. We'd always been equal. So I wanted to get back to that. And it was a really strong motivation. Just to get good at something and prove that I can be good at something, I can earn money, I can get back to where I was. I thought, OK, well the lesson here is that I have to try and change track. I wanted a career, I wanted this to be the start of something.

'For the longest time when I didn't have a job, I would just look at other people. I'd look at people on the bus. I'd look at people on the pavements. I'd think they're all going off to a meeting or they're going to an office. They've all got somewhere to go and they're all busy. They're earning money. I don't know what it is they're doing but I could probably do it. I just want that job. I don't know what that job is. I just want the job. I want a career.

'All my skills and experience pointed to teaching. I chatted to friends and some of my husband's friends who were teachers who said, "Well, you know, you've got all the skills and experience to be a teacher." It kept happening and I started to think, well, that would seem obvious. That's what you've got the ability to do, it doesn't really matter that that's not what you are passionate about, maybe that's what you should do.

'And obviously, I didn't have a professional qualification. But I wrote a lovely letter to a school explaining that I had been out of work for the best part of five years, but I hadn't just been out of work. I'd been learning about my kids, about other kids, about how kids learn through play. And hosting playgroups, all sorts of things I'd been up to.

'I did have to work quite hard at the job interview. They were testing me out with questions. And I was just drawing on examples of things I'd done with my own kids. I wanted them to see that the things that I do at home, I could do them in this job and I'd be perfect. I remember walking out of the interview, and I walked through the school reception, and my phone started ringing in the bottom of my bag. I'm not a very poised person, and the phone was ringing and ringing and of course I'd left my kids for the day and I was panicked. I couldn't find my phone in my bag and then I was on my hands and knees and had raisins, tissues, everything in the reception of the school, and then finally I got the phone out of my bag. And it was the woman who'd just interviewed me saying you know what, you've got the job. They could have looked through the window and seen me on my hands and knees!'

After a year as a classroom assistant, Kerys signed up for a PGCE to get her formal teaching qualification, helped by money from her parents. It was a hard year, balancing study and family. But it was a move she feels has made real sense for her situation.

'You know when you go to a job interview and they say why do you want the job? I know a good answer isn't "Well, you know, it's really practical. I can't get a job in journalism and I want the school holidays." But for me that was what was behind it. And then you learn to like it after that. You know, as you get good at it. You learn to become passionate about it. I mean, I do get the holidays with my kids but I really do feel it's one of those careers where it's never stagnant, you're constantly learning, it's a fulfilling job. The first year of teaching is really, really hard but it's so worth it, it all pays off. Because you have a great job that you can go to different countries and use, and there's loads of opportunities once you're a teacher to not do the same thing all the time. You know, you can specialize, you can go to a different school, you can teach different kinds of kids. It's endlessly worth it.

'My advice to someone is to really think about what you value most, and I really valued, and really wanted to be an equal contributor to, the family – that was a real driving force for me. I also wanted to have something for me. I think I want to be good at something. I don't just want to be someone's mum. I want to have my own identity.'

JANETTE, forties
Police Officer to Furniture Creator

'I do try and sit back and reflect on what I've achieved. And when I look back over the last 18 months, it is massive. I have to pinch myself and think have I really done that? And there is a bit of sadness. What could I have achieved had I done this a lot sooner?'

Janette has worked as a police officer for 27 years, she suspects inspired by the old-fashioned police houses across the road from where she grew up and her experiences of being bullied at school, which motivated her to 'make things right for people'. She climbed the career ladder, married a fellow officer and had two children. Her story involves the collision of a long-expected need for a career change with a lockdown hobby. Unlike Kerys, Janette is a definite advocate of the find-your-passion school of career change. What about you? She's also a great example of a change that involves a slow transition period and has advice to share from her entrepreneurial journey and her battle with imposter syndrome.

'There wasn't much part-time work in the police and it's really hard with a family. I've always felt a bit restless really. I do sort of a look back and think, would I change it? I probably wouldn't do it again now. I've dealt with some quite horrible things. I've also had some really good jobs though, and a great sense of satisfaction, but there is more to life.'

In Janette's case, the 'more to life' question has been hovering for some time, as her long service entitles her to retire from the police at fifty in just a few years' time.

'Fifty is too young to retire, so my thoughts have always been around what else to do. At the minute, my role in the police is around financial investigation and fraud, which is lucrative in the private sector, far better paid than the police. I looked at going down that route, or shifting to a civilian job, but to be honest I wanted to do something totally different. I'd had enough of the restriction. Not the discipline exactly, but the police service is very black and white, so to speak. And I've done all my long hours, I've done all the trauma and I wanted something totally different.'

That something different has emerged from a hobby, a real case of a passion turned career.

'Lockdown gave me that opportunity to sort of slow things down. I had literally just painted my kitchen – that was a lockdown project – and then, after a glass or two of Prosecco, I told my husband I was going to paint a sideboard! So I bought one for about £40 off Marketplace and I sold it to a couple in the West Country six weeks later for £500. By the time I'd got home (I forgot to factor in delivery!), they'd emailed me to say they wanted another one. I did a few more pieces. I think I did about seven or eight and they all sold within two weeks. So it was like, well, where do I go from here?'

What started as a release from a stressful job has turned into a business over the last two years. So how did Janette investigate this Future Me?

'I first learnt the techniques online and then I found some local courses and just went and did a two-hour painting class with a lady who does furniture. Then I came across a group online run by a brilliant furniture artist and I joined her subscription group. It's an amazing group of artists and I learnt lots that way.

'I haven't had to invest a lot financially from the outset, that was important. I've built it up gradually. It's been about learning the business. I used to think, well, how many pieces do I have to have before I can open my shop on Etsy? And how many . . . but no, just do it. If it doesn't work out, what's the worst thing that can happen? And there are a lot of free things, free advice – local councils run business courses and that sort of thing. And building a network is helpful. There are quite a few different groups on Facebook for furniture and upcycling, communities which are so supportive. There's not a question you couldn't ask in the group, you know, around setting up your Etsy store, setting up your website, marketing techniques. And that's only a small monthly membership outlay. Now I'm in the position where I'm starting to outsource things like marketing and photos. But again, I joined another group online, it isn't a massive subscription, but when I finish a piece of furniture I then photograph it, send the photo to America, they edit it and send it back again. And I've now got myself an accountant because I want to be able to put my profits back into growing the business.'

For Janette, it's all about this period of transition. She has sought permission to condense her hours, working four longer days, Monday to Thursday, in the police, where she is no longer on the front line, and then Friday, Saturday, Sunday and evenings on her growing business.

'It is a lot of work because at times I feel I have two full-time jobs. But I'm fortunate in that I've got the family support around me in terms of help and my kids are grown up – and you know the house isn't as tidy as it used to be. I don't go to the gym as much as I used to do. Things have had to give, but I just want to go for it really!'

In fact, her furniture business is so successful it could already provide all the work Janette needs. When we speak, she's recently attended the *Grand Designs* exhibition in London. But her pension arrangements mean she needs to see out her time with the police, so her career transition will last several years.

Meanwhile she is getting to grips with her new self and the imposter syndrome that sometimes creeps in to career change.

'That's the biggest thing. I do have to frequently have conversations with myself. When people speak to me, they think I'm an expert, because this is my field and I'm a professional, but I know I'm a beginner. Clearly there is some talent there and I can clearly do the job, but you have to wing it sometimes! I liken it to my first shift out on patrol as a police officer. It was a late shift in June in Blackpool and there were thousands of people and I thought, oh my God, what have I done? There's a 20-year-old thinking I've got to walk down here in uniform, what if people talk to me? And it's a bit like that. But when you get the feedback from people, that's what spurs me on.'

What does Janette want from her career change? What is her Why?

'I think it's freedom – getting that quality of life and getting the flexibility. I think it's headspace. It's really therapeutic. Obviously being in the police is not an easy job and it does affect you mentally, so the painting is different. And I think it's a sense of achievement. It's down to me. I've worked for people all my life and there are so many external pressures and political pressures around policing. But my business is down to me and it's a real sense of achievement for me. And I'm dealing with nice people all the time!

'For me it's been about finding the passion, I suppose. There's an expression, isn't there? Find a thing you love and you'll never work a day in your life. It's finding a passion that doesn't feel like hard work.

'I do try and sit back and reflect on what I've achieved. And when I look back over the last 18 months, it is massive. I have to pinch myself and think have I really done that? And there is a bit of sadness. What could I have achieved had I done this a lot sooner? I think one of my big passions is around how your opportunities and experiences at school really form what you go on to do in later life. I still remember my art teacher laughing at me, telling me I wasn't very creative. And actually, since then, I had never done anything and it was only really in lockdown that I picked up a paintbrush. I mean, I'd done DIY, but now I'm kicking myself because I just wish I could have tuned into my creativity more as a child and I might have done something totally different.'

You can see Janette's work on Instagram here: @petunias_attic

An Injection of Commitment, Courage and Curiosity

I always ask my clients for the most powerful lessons they learnt along their career change journey. Here are ten crackers! Use these when you just need a blast of encouragement from someone who's done it.

1. You need to look at the bigger picture and not get too tied into the details too early.

2. Remember that you are probably the biggest advocate for your own limitations. You can flip that around and advocate for your own unique abilities!

3. With a structure, you can cut through what sometimes feels like the molasses of your own thoughts. By giving yourself time to think and talk things through, either on your own or with friends, you can chip away, develop a plan and solve your challenges.

4. Small steps lead to other steps. This is a process that might take some time but it is constantly changing and reshaping, and you can direct it in the best possible way for you and your interests.

5. You have a good network and should use it.

6. It's all about the power of people and how things only change when you take action.

7. Change is possible! You are not alone and your situation and the feelings connected to it are not exceptional.

8. You can do things you set your mind to. You'll learn that a lot of your doubts and worries are based on fear. You need to ask yourself the right questions to get past what you initially assume is wrong to what is actually wrong.

9. You have the energy and skills to move forwards – you just have to believe that and take action.

10. You just need to get off your bum and stop overthinking!

Resources

Chapter 3: What You're Good At

Personality Profiles

https://www.16personalities.com/

You could also experiment with a different test at
https://www.truity.com/

Cliftonstrengths offers a paid version, should you want to invest
more time (and some money!) here:
https://www.gallup.com/cliftonstrengths/en/253868/popular-
cliftonstrengths-assessment-products.aspx

Chapter 5: How You Want to Work

Financial Planning Tools

https://www.moneysavingexpert.com/banking/budget-planning/

https://www.citizensadvice.org.uk/debt-and-money/budgeting/
budgeting/work-out-your-budget/budgeting-tool

Chapter 7: Capturing and Generating Ideas

Job Websites

https://www.monster.co.uk/

https://uk.indeed.com/

https://www.totaljobs.com/

https://jobs.theguardian.com/

https://www.adzuna.co.uk/

https://www.reed.co.uk/

https://www.escapethecity.org/

Chapter 9: Trying On Your Future Mes

Massive Open Online Courses

https://www.edx.org

https://www.futurelearn.com/

https://www.coursera.org

https://theskillstoolkit.campaign.gov.uk

https://www.udemy.com

https://www.open.edu/openlearn/

https://www.linkedin.com/learning/

Masterclasses/Workshops

https://howtoacademy.com/

https://www.theguardian.com/guardian-masterclasses

https://www.eventbrite.co.uk/

Interest Groups

https://www.meetup.com/

Facebook

To discover new groups you might be interested in:

From your News Feed, click Groups in the left menu.

Put some keywords into the Search function (children's therapist, horse lovers, women in HR) or click Discover to see Suggested for you, Friends' groups, Categories, Popular near you or More suggestions.

LinkedIn

You can search for groups by name or keyword, or you can browse groups recommended for you by LinkedIn.

> To search for groups by name or keyword: Enter your keyword or group name in the Search bar at the top of your LinkedIn homepage. Select (group name) Groups from the dropdown.

> To browse for groups recommended for you by LinkedIn: Click the Work icon in the top right of your LinkedIn homepage and select Groups from the menu that appears. Scroll down to the bottom of the page and click Search.

Volunteering

Volunteer organizations:

> https://reachvolunteering.org.uk/

> https://volunteeringmatters.org.uk/

> https://doit.life/volunteer

To take your skills on to a board or work as a charity trustee:

> https://www.gettingonboard.org/

> https://www.womenonboards.net/en-gb/home.aspx

To be a school governor:

> https://www.inspiringgovernance.org/volunteers/

> https://www.nga.org.uk/Governance-Recruitment/Be-a-school-governor-or-trustee.aspx

To work as a magistrate:

> https://www.gov.uk/become-magistrate/apply-to-be-a-magistrate

Chapter 10: Really Doing It

Returnships

https://inclusivity.co.uk/

https://womenreturners.com/

https://www.thereturnhub.com/ (for careers in financial services)

Acknowledgements

When an email appeared in my inbox from Fenella Bates at
Penguin asking if I might be interested in writing a book, I was so
surprised I went straight to LinkedIn to see if Fenella was a real
person or if this was some dodgy scam.

If ever there were proof of my assertion that expanding your
world leads to interesting opportunities, it was my decision to be
brave and ask Lorraine Candy and Trish Halpin if I could appear
on their brilliant podcast *Postcards from Midlife*. My first thanks
must go to them – our discussion on reinventing your work in
later life was heard by Fenella and a chain of events began that
has culminated in this book.

Eighteen months on, I can happily confirm that Fenella is not
just a real person but a wise, energetic and supportive editor who
has guided me through an unfamiliar process and provided more
evidence that – even at forty-six – new things are always possible.
So my thanks to Fenella and the skilled team at Penguin Michael
Joseph who have brought the *Career Change Guide* to life including
Paula Flanagan, Emma Henderson, Emma Horton and Fran
Monteiro.

A big thank you too to the many wonderful clients and career
changers who shared their experiences with me so honestly and
openly and allowed me to tell them to you.

It was the team at Firework Career Coaching who set me

on my journey to help people reshape their working lives and who now, as colleagues, remain a valued source of inspiration, reflection and encouragement. I am hugely grateful. As I am to other friends in the coaching community who never fail to offer support and insight.

Finally, to my husband, Jeremy, whose enthusiasm and energy for his work inspires me daily, and to our daughters, Martha and Anna, who will soon set out on their own exciting career adventures – thank you for the pep talks, the cups of tea and the unwavering belief/eye-rolls when I started to doubt.

You see – the magic really is in the people . . .

Index